NUPTSE (7861m)

NUPTSE
WEST

LHOTSE (8501m)

LHOTSE FACE

CWM

DARK SHADOWS
FALLING

SOUTH FACE OF PUMORI

································ CZECH ROUTE
━━━━━━━━━━━━ NORMAL ROUTE
━ ━ ━ ━ ━ ━ ━ ━ SIMPSON/DELANEY '96 ATTEMPT

DARK
SHADOWS
FALLING

Joe Simpson

THE MOUNTAINEERS
Seattle

by the same author
TOUCHING THE VOID
(winner of the Boardman Tasker Award and the NCR Award)
THE WATER PEOPLE
THIS GAME OF GHOSTS
STORMS OF SILENCE

First published in the United Kingdom in 1997 by Jonathan Cape,

Random House, 20 Vauxhall Bridge Road, London SW1V 2SA

This edition published in 1997 in the United States of America by
The Mountaineers, 1001 SW Klickitat Way, Seattle WA 98134

Library of Congress
Cataloging-in-Publication Data

A catalog record for this book
is available at the Library of Congress

ISBN 0-89886-549-2 (United States)

Typeset by MATS, Southend-on-Sea, Essex

Contents

Illustrations

Endpaper: The south side of Mount Everest.
Frontispiece: The new and normal routes up Pumori.

Between pages 64 and 65:

Between pages 144 and 145:

. . . what is Everest without the eye that sees it?
It is the hearts of men that make it big or small.

Tenzing Norgay, in *Man of Everest*
(as told to James Ramsey Ullman)

INTRODUCTION

Dead Man Moving

A bitter wind raked across the shattered rocks of Mount Everest's South Col, brushing gritty snow into the folds of a dying man's clothing. He lay on his back with his bare hands resting at his sides. Less than a rope's length away, in a huddle of tents, seven men slept in snug sleeping bags. The dying man had lain outside for many hours, exposed to a withering wind.

His mind collapsed slowly as his body went through the motions of living. The system began closing down, rationalising away the luxuries of digits and limbs and non-vital organs, protecting the core until all that was left was the core. Viscous blood cooled in deadened limbs as his body temperature kept dropping by steady fractions of degrees. Limbs abandoned to save the core hardened like chicken thighs in a deep freeze; flesh became death-coloured, bluish grey to off-white, and solid. Chilled blood cannot return to cool the core. That was all he had become – a fragile core, an imperceptible pulse in lifeless flesh. It was a very long death.

A few metres short of eight thousand metres high, the South Col is a bleak strip of level ground suspended between the great summits of Everest and Lhotse. In places it is strewn with shattered rocks and bounded on each side by the vast icy drops down the Lhotse and Kangshung Faces. Over the years it has become littered with the detritus of countless expeditions, remnants of torn tents, wind-fractured tent poles, abandoned empty oxygen bottles, here and there the frozen corpses of unsuccessful climbers. It is the site of the last camp climbers make before their attempt on the summit in a long day's climb up from the Col.

This man had long since forgotten what he was doing, why he was there in the freezing windy night. The urgent signals warning of cold, and exhaustion, and collapse had faded away as if somehow his mind had accepted that he was now beyond recall; as if an orderly, rational retreat from the complicated business of staying alive had begun. For him it was like sleep, embraced with a resigned weary spirit. Perhaps he was filled with a sense of helplessness; perhaps he felt a sad and crushing loneliness, or maybe a flare of anger made feeble in the chill of the night. Even these thoughts faded as the cold took him slowly down, and he could do nothing about it. A deep resignation washed over him. Loss of consciousness was a silence that soothed away the pain of trying to live as he lay among the shattered rocks, glad that it was finished.

He had no understanding of anything any more, and was even unaware of when he had sunk to his knees for the last time, then slumped on to the icy rocks and rolled on to his back. Staring blankly at the darkness above him, unable to register what he was seeing, he lay for five hours as an endless night sky swept over him. He tried to conjure up some reason for it all but his mind had ceased to function. It no longer meant anything to him that he was on the highest mountain in the world. His memory of that terrible day, which had started with his companions so very long ago was hazy, disconnected. What had happened, where they had all gone was beyond knowing.

He could not remember becoming separated from his companions. In the storm they had spread out as they fought to reach their camp on the Col. At least one of the others was also dying that night, hanging slumped against the snow on the fixed ropes below the Col, unable to move up or down, resigned to the same slow dying.

The climber lying on the Col never realised how close he had come to being saved. It was a mercy of sorts. For a moment at the end of the long night hands had pulled at him, voices harried him, frozen fingers had groped vainly for his fluttering pulse, felt for the slightest zephyr of damp breath at his lips. Then he was alone again, unaware that others on the Col had found him and then left him for dead.

He lay on his back, teased by the killing wind as if it were trying to wake him, tugging insistently at his side. He could not recall when he had removed his gloves, his chilled brain sending confused automatic responses, convincing him that he was too hot, but it didn't matter because his hands and even his forearms were lost now. Had he been able to concentrate he might have heard the flexing and flapping sounds of the wind harrying the nylon of the Dutch tents less than thirty yards from where he lay. In the darkness he might have understood what the noise meant – comfort, warmth, companionship. Perhaps the familiar sound had stirred something in his frozen memory, or the recognition of voices drifting over from the tents into his fading consciousness had triggered the almost superhuman effort to wave one hand. A feeble, slow wave. A plea. *Help me. Hold me, please.* Whatever signal pulsed through his enfeebled body, slowly his arm began to move. The effort in itself should have killed him as the chilled blood released by the spasms of his arm rushed back to his precious core. Either way, it was too late for him, and he died within reach of sanctuary.

The Sherpa who had struggled out of his tent to relieve himself stared in horror at the bare, frozen, waving hand. The dark edge of night had retreated to the gradated cloud layers of the horizon. It was the beginning of a harsh blustery day. A desolate, ashen sky of lowering clouds hung over the Col, but there was no doubting what he could see. It was a dead man moving. A shock of superstitious fear bolted through him as he scrabbled at the zipped tent door, shouting for someone to help him. There was a dead man moving and he wanted to get inside quickly.

A confused chatter of voices rose and fell in volume as the wind snatched away the questions that were shouted between the tents. In a tense uneasy atmosphere, the zip on a tent door was eased down and a wide-eyed face peered out at the body with the waving hand and then ducked quickly back inside, to be replaced by another frightened staring expression.

There was the disjointed crackle of a radio, squelch noises, scattered bursts of white noise, an urgent request for acknowledgement – *'Hello Base camp, Camp IV here, can I speak to Janneke? Do you read me?'* – as outside the arm slowly waved to the now closed and zippered tents. Voices, raised in disbelief, demanded explanations from the radio.

'Hello? There is a body outside which still moves. Is it possible for a dead body to make uncontrolled movements? Can dead men move? Over.'

'No! That's impossible, but it is possible for a live body to move. Over.'

A surreal conversation with team doctors at base camp thousands of metres below crackled across the windy desolation of the South Col. *Could he be alive? If he is alive, could he survive? So if we cannot save him, then he is a dead man...is there nothing we can do for him?*

So they didn't go out to hold the dying man, to still his piteous waving arm with a gentle hand. No one took his pulse or checked his vital signs. No one acknowledged his last despairing movement, knelt by him and had the humanity to hug him. He died alone as his fate was discussed earnestly in a bizarre radio call. They let him die alone for reasons best known to themselves. Perhaps they did not want to face his dying; maybe the finality of it was too intimidating for them to face.

1

Dying Values

In May 1992 Deepak Kulkani and Raymond Jacob with one, perhaps two other members of the somewhat disorganised Indian Civil Expedition left Camp III on the Lhotse face and made an abortive attempt to get to the South Col on Everest in a day of strong winds and intense cold. By nightfall they still had not reached the Col, where another group of Indian climbers – from the Indo-Tibetan Border Police – were already camped. Nearby were the tents of a Dutch expedition, led by Ronald Naar, and their Sherpas. In his book, *Alleen De Top Telt (Only the Summit Counts)*, Naar states that in the night he heard 'a fearful scream above the sound of the roaring wind'. A short while later another chilling scream reached the ears of the Dutch team and one of the Sherpas went out to look for the source. He found nothing.

According to Naar, the leader of his neighbouring Indian team came over for a discussion. He too had heard the cries and had searched the area without finding anyone. Persuading themselves that they were mistaken, they retired to their sleeping bags, satisfied with their perfunctory searches.

At first light, about six o'clock, a female member of the Indian Border Police expedition visited the Dutch tents to report that they had a 'casualty' and needed help. When asked what sort of help was required, the Indian climber hesitated before others from the Indian team appeared and said that the victim had died. Naar writes that the woman, named as Santosh, was in some confusion about what had happened. She tells him: 'My colleagues gave him oxygen to revive him but now he is beyond help they say. He is already dead it seems.'

15

'But what has happened?' Naar asks her.

'I have no idea. But the others have decided to go down.'

The Indian team and their Sherpas then left the South Col and descended towards the Western Cwm with what strikes me as unseemly haste. A few questions occurred to me immediately. If someone is dead, why try to administer oxygen to him? Was the man actually dead when the Indians said he *'was beyond help'* or was he in their opinion as good as dead? Either way, their behaviour, both in their attempts at search and rescue and the speed with which they abandoned their dead or dying countryman, seems to me to be pretty poor. The Dutch had no reason to believe that the man was anything other than dead and didn't bother to check the body lying close to their tents. For them, it would be unimaginable to think that anyone might abandon a living team member. In fact it wasn't, as Naar seems to suppose, one of their neighbours but a missing climber from the other team who had set out from Camp III the previous day. Clearly the anguished screams in the night had not been imagined.

The retreating Indians then came across the frozen corpse of Deepak Kulkani clipped to the fixed ropes leading up from Camp III to the South Col. He too must have become lost, disorientated by the stormy night conditions, and by a state of collapse. Hypothermia and exhaustion had killed him some time during the night. Perhaps it was his screams everyone had heard – pitiful cries for help from a man lost and exhausted in the darkness, groping for some sign of the tents. We shall never know.

In their swift descent from the Col the Indians simply left him hanging on the rope. To me, this seems somewhat insensitive. Edmond Oefner, one of the Dutch climbers, was to say later how they were consequently forced to climb over the man's body on later ascents to the Col until someone eventually cut him free in the hope that he would fall into the Western Cwm. Unfortunately the body became jammed in rocks a short distance below the ropes. It appears that no further effort was made to bury or retrieve the body. Neither was any attempt made to cover or bury the body of the Indian lying on the Col. Perhaps it would be too cynical to suggest that they might have known he wasn't dead when they left – simply '*beyond help*', and hence unburied.

Meanwhile, the Dutch had a brief discussion about what they wanted to do. The weather was too cold and windy for a summit attempt that day. They knew that to stay on the Col would be a heavy drain on their strength and resilience. A quick retreat to Camp II in the Western Cwm, to recuperate and wait for an improvement in the conditions, was obviously the better idea, but for the moment they prevaricated. Settling back into their sleeping bags, they rested for the next four hours until one of their Sherpas crawled outside to relieve himself. He was soon back, pale-faced and visibly shaken.

'There is a dead body waving over there,' he says to a startled Ronald Naar. The Dutch leader peers out of the tent and sees the body lying amidst the snow-drifted rocks. Every now and then one of the man's arms comes up very slowly in an eerie sort of salute before it is lowered slowly back to his side. There was indeed a dead man waving.

One might have expected it to be their instinctive reaction to rush to the poor man's aid; to try to get him under cover and maybe revive him with oxygen and fluids. After all, he was only between twenty and thirty metres from the their tents. There were five Dutch climbers and two Sherpas in residence on the Col, sufficient to get the man into a tent. Instead there followed a bizarre radio conversation between Ronald Naar and the expedition doctor at base camp. Having established that dead men cannot make involuntary movements, Naar asked about the man's physical condition. The experts at base camp advised him that since the man had lain exposed to the fury of the elements for so long, it would be quite impossible to revive him or do anything to save him. This may very well be true, but it could only really be verified by a physical examination of the victim. No one made any attempt to do this.

On discovering that the Indian was alive and waving, the two Sherpas were distressed by what had happened, convinced in a fatalistic way that a man returning from the dead was a serious omen.

'He is a dead man and he calls us,' Nima tells Naar. 'Our

religion says a calling dead man means we should follow. We too must die.'

The Sherpas wanted to descend as soon as possible. One of the Dutch climbers, Hans Anterbosch, was also adamant that he wanted to leave. Naar left his tent to go to the adjacent tent and discuss the situation, glancing across as he went at the silent figure lying on his back, waving feebly. Ray Delaney translated their conversation for me three years after the event as I sat in his front room in Holland watching a video of the expedition that had been shown on Dutch television. No one went to examine the victim. In the shelter and relative comfort of their tent the Dutch climbers come to the conclusion that the core temperature of the man lying outside must be so low that to do anything – move him, feed him fluids or try to administer oxygen – would almost certainly kill him. The man had lain there since possibly as early as one thirty in the morning after climbing all day in stormy conditions – nearly nine hours exposed to the killing wind. It was now four hours since the Indian Border Police climbers had pronounced him dead. After Hans and another Dutch climber had left with the Sherpas, the remaining three filmed each other discussing what should be done. I watched their video in hushed despair, thinking all the time of the poor man dying alone barely a rope's length from the nylon walls in the background. They did not go outside again until the three Dutch climbers made their attempt on the summit, the next day stepping past the man's body on their way. They were forced to retreat some hundred metres below the South Summit.

At the end of the video I was shocked and angry at what I had seen. For me, it seemed as pernicious an example of pragmatic, self-serving callousness as I had ever heard in the mountains. Sadly, I have heard worse since, but at the time I could not recall any comparable behaviour in mountaineering history, and furthermore I was astonished that such a distressing story hadn't appeared in any of the international climbing journals. Until 1997 I don't believe the story had been published outside of the Netherlands.

I found it astounding that the Dutch made no attempt to examine the dying Indian. In truth, all that the base camp doctors could do over the radio was to speculate on the man's condition and, however well meant this may have been, it was never going to be more than guesswork. It was enough to justify Ronald Naar's insistence that his duty was not to put the safety of his team at risk in any attempt to save the man. The decision, it might be noted, also meant that they could pursue an unsuccessful summit attempt the following day.

In the spring of 1996, a year after I had watched the Naar video, a deadly storm swept across the summit region of Everest, with tragic results. Eight climbers died during one night and later the following day, but many more survived the horrendous conditions. The laudable behaviour of both victims and rescuers stands out in stark contrast to the expediency of the decision taken by Ronald Naar. In the storm, an American climber, Beck Weathers, was abandoned by rescuers who were overwhelmed by the conditions and the number of victims needing help. They simply couldn't find him in the dark and assumed that he must be dead. Having slumped in a comatose state, the American revived many hours later in daylight and staggered to the safety of the tents on the Col. He suffered severe frostbite injuries, with the loss of his right hand and part of his nose, but otherwise was physically healthy. He had spent more than thirty hours at or above the Col, without oxygen for most of that time, and had survived through a long night of ferocious winds and plummeting temperatures. He was alive despite suffering considerably more trauma than the Indian climber in 1992. Close to Beck Weathers a Japanese woman, Yasuko Namba, had been found and abandoned, believed dead. She did not survive.

The weather that night was appalling, with blizzard white-out and freezing temperatures that were far more extreme than the relatively benign conditions in 1992. Rescue attempts were conducted in the stormy darkness of the night at distances from the tents far in excess of the thirty yards that separated the Indian climber from safety and warmth. The following day a Taiwanese climber, Makalu Gau, was revived and rescued from a forced open bivouac over a thousand feet above Camp IV on the Col. He lost all his fingers, thumbs and toes from frostbite but nevertheless survived. A well-known American guide, Scott Fischer, was found unconscious at his side, but he could not be revived and rescued.

These examples show clearly what utter nonsense it is to act upon a medical prognosis made in base camp as to the life expectancy of anyone on the South Col without first making a physical examination. When the victim is a stone's throw away and you have warmth, shelter, oxygen, food and seven people capable of helping, then failure to go and take a close look at him seems to be more than a little negligent.

In Ronald Naar's account of the events on the Col there is a distinct lack of emotion. Pragmatism seems to have been the order of the day.

'That man walked into his own death,' Naar writes in *Alleen de Top Telt (Only the Summit Counts)*. 'I don't want any of us to get hurt. It makes no sense to try to rescue him.'

'But he is still human. He still lives, and we have to do something, don't we?' Hans van Meulen cries out in despair. Naar is adamant that nothing should be done; and his view prevails. It is too dangerous, he says, and although he understands their distress, he insists that nothing be done. 'If anyone accuses us later, you can always say I was responsible,' he tells his companions.

'Both our eyes point to the ground, ashamed,' he writes – a strange remark, which seems to be an admission of having done something wrong.

I watched the video taken the following day of the body, now dead, lying on its back in a red duvet jacket, wearing neoprene over-boots, the bare hands visible, and the sound of the cameraman's strangely familiar voice crying and swearing in despair. I learned later that the cameraman was Edmond Oefner, a friend of mine from my climbing days in the Alps. It was a shock to learn this. Edmond was a kind man, a friendly, smiling, cheerful man who loved life and living – someone whom I would always have relied upon to comfort anyone in distress. I found it difficult to understand why he had gone along with Naar's decision. He had never struck me as likely to allow himself to be bullied into doing things of which he strongly disapproved.

'I thought you'd be surprised,' Ray said, interrupting my

shocked silence as the video clicked to an end. 'Not good, eh?'

'I can't believe it,' I said, shaking my head.

'Here,' Ray said, handing me another beer. 'What can you say? These things happen, I suppose.'

'No, they don't,' I snapped. 'Not unless you let them.'

'Yeah, I know, but what can be done?' Ray shrugged. 'It's a bloody circus out there.'

'What? On Everest, you mean?'

'Mainly, but the whole thing's going belly up now. It's a joke.'

'Yeah, maybe ... well, why are you coming to Pumori then?'

'Because you asked me, and I'd forgotten about this,' he said, nodding towards the television set on which he had shown the video.

'Forgot! How could you forget that?' I took a drag on my cigarette, sucking the smoke deep into my lungs, and then exhaled in a long sigh. 'You know what I can't understand?'

'What?'

'Well, why did they all go along with it? I'm amazed at Edmond. It just seems so out of character.'

'Why not ask him? You've got his phone number, haven't you?'

'Yeah, but he gave it to me twelve years ago, I doubt if it'll be the same now,' I murmured. 'And anyway, what the hell do I say to him?'

'That's your problem.' He shrugged and grinned at me.

Some months later, having built up the nerve to ask some painful questions, I called the number and discovered that Edmond was still living at the same address. He was as friendly as ever, and quite happy to talk to me about the events on the South Col, not in the least wary when I asked if I could record the conversation for future use. If he had had some terrible secret to hide, I doubt that he would have even considered speaking to me about it, let alone allowing me to record the conversation.

'I realise it was an appalling position to find yourself in,' I said at last, 'and a terrible decision to have to make, but couldn't you have done *something*?'

'It was impossible. We discussed everything we might do for him, fluids, warming up, medicines, but there was nothing we could do. He looked truly awful, very blue, half covered in snow and very stiff already. The doctors had said that the moment we moved him he would die because his core temperature was so low. What could we do? It was minus twenty degrees in the tents!'

'Maybe I'm just being emotional,' I replied, 'but couldn't someone have comforted him, held his hand so he could sense that he was not alone?'

'Afterwards, actually, it was the only thing I thought perhaps I should have had the guts to do. I should have done it, but I couldn't . . . I know maybe I could have gone over and put my big gloved hand on him, and said sorry friend, but in that situation we could not do it. It is hard to describe . . . it is like this Indian man is the body of your fear, do you understand?'

'What you're saying is it would scare you to confront his dying?'

'I was scared, at 8000 metres, and this man dying out there. It was the most fearsome thing you can think in the mountains. And we felt almost as helpless as the man himself. I didn't want to take death in my hands, Joe. I think that is as fair as I can be about it.'

'Yes, and I suppose I feel as I do because I have been in a really bad situation. I was left for dead once, and I know how lonely that felt. It is the loneliness that I remember most, and that's why I kept fighting. If I was to die, I knew I had to find somebody to be with. That is why I feel so strongly that someone should have held that man.'

'Yes, but it's so hard,' Edmond told me.

There was nothing really that I could say. I wasn't there, and I cannot be certain how I would have behaved in similar circumstances, though I can make a very good guess. I was left with the uncomfortable suspicion that, had the dying man been Dutch, they might not have behaved in the same way. Would their public profile at home have been damaged irreparably, I wondered, if they had treated a fellow country-man in this manner? Could they honestly say that if the dying man had been a close friend, a brother, a wife, a lover, they would *not* have gone out and held him in their arms? If they would have behaved differently in these circumstances, then it seems to me that they might have been distressingly selective about the way they behaved towards the dying stranger.

I can only guess at how close I came to dying in Peru in 1985 when Simon Yates cut the rope and I plunged into the crevasse on Siula Grande. I have spoken to a number of doctors since, all of whom have suggested that, given the circumstances, I should have died. Although there was a lot of pain and anguish and hardship during the four days in which I struggled to survive, it is the dreadful loneliness that still deeply unsettles me. Much of what I did at that time was instinctive; or due to experience, but what kept me going for so long when all seemed lost was the desperate desire for company. I went beyond caring whether I lived or died so long as I did not have to die alone. I wanted a hand to hold, a voice to hear. I craved for some human contact that might alleviate the terrifying emptiness of those days spent slowly dying.

Of course, death is the one thing we will all face alone, even if surrounded by thousands, and I now have some idea of what dying will be like. Because I felt myself balanced on the edge of nothingness, I have already partly died, and I don't look forward to the day when I have to do it again. Because of that, I think I have some sense of what the Indian climber on the South Col may have experienced. A little imagination and a degree of compassion is all any of us needs to understand his plight.

In the past I have been exhausted to the point of carelessness on mountains, cold enough to feel myself drifting down into a pain-free sleep, a black hole calling me, lost in time, like death, and felt myself accepting it without concern or remorse. I have stared into darkness and cried in despair; wept because I was alone, because there was no one there. I have also known the indescribable relief of hearing a voice in the night, of seeing the saccharine yellow beam of a torch come searching for me, of hearing footsteps rushing towards me and the comforting feel of strong arms pulling me into warmth and safety, and of knowing that I was not alone any more. At very least, I can empathise with that poor man on the South Col, imagine myself in his position all too clearly. The thought that he got so close to company, to a helping hand and a caring voice, and yet was rejected, sends a cold shiver down my spine. I cannot conceive of anything more dreadful, nor imagine a greater sense of despair. In truth, I find it hard to believe that anyone could behave so callously as to ignore him, deprive him of a caring presence.

Looking back rationally now as a mountaineer, I can see no reason why Simon Yates should have attempted to rescue me. Indeed, at the time I really thought it to be an impossible task, and if that were so then any such attempt would be suicidal. I was six thousand metres up a remote mountain with a badly shattered knee. We had run out of food and gas that morning and there were no mountain rescue teams or helicopters to call upon. As a two-man team, climbing Alpine-style with no other climbers in the vicinity, we always knew that even a minor accident could be a death sentence. Suddenly we were forced to confront a situation of our own making, one that we had hoped would never happen. We found ourselves in a game that no one was likely to win – so much so that it became how we strove to play the game that counted in the end.

When the testing moment came, I looked into the eyes of a friend and wondered what he was thinking, what he was going to do, whether he would leave me to die or help me. It seemed to take a very long time while my life hung in the balance of another man's thoughts.

Simon had a way out. I did not. It would have been quite reasonable for him to climb down alone, leaving me to my fate. No one would have any right to criticise him for such a course of action. He would probably have been able to descend the mountain safely on his own, although it would have been an extreme undertaking. He might have softened the blow by telling me that he was going to get help (which of course he and I knew didn't exist), and I would have felt frightened and abandoned, but I could have understood that he had no other choice. I would probably have tried to believe the white lie about getting help just to make things easier and give myself a flicker of hope.

Some readers of *Touching the Void* (my book about the incident) have written to me saying how brave I must be – which is flattering but untrue. Simon was brave, very brave. He had a choice and bravery cannot exist if there are no such options. Fighting your way out of a burning house is not brave, simply sensible. Going into a burning house to save someone when you can choose not to do so is brave, although sometimes foolhardy. Simon chose to try to rescue me single-handed, an audacious and exceptional piece of mountaineering requiring skill, experience beyond his years and, above all, courage. In the end he succeeded, albeit in an indirect and rather protracted manner.

It is a mistake to believe that some people have a stronger will to live than others. I believe that it is not in our nature to give up easily. Usually what dictates whether we survive or not are the particular circumstances and the skills and experience that enable us to cope with the situation. More often than not, survival is simply a matter of chance. The fact that the survivor keeps on fighting does not imply that those who die in similar circumstances do not try just as hard. They may be less fortunate, or less physically and mentally equipped to deal with their predicament, but they will all have fought to survive. We humans are not more stubborn as a species than other creatures, nor are we endowed with some indefinable will; it is simply a matter of instinct built into every creature, like breathing.

What we do possess are intellect and imagination which enable us to conceive of a future beyond our present plight and to draw hope and comfort from the prospect of a better existence at a time when our suffering will be over.

It is ironic, then, that so many who would never think of venturing up high mountains have found something uplifting and positive in our survival on Siula Grande. Of course I can see why for others there is something of a life-affirming aspect to the story. It affirms the encouraging and hopeful thought that if you keep trying, despite the odds stacked against you, then you can succeed. If you never give up, it is possible to pull through. In some ways it becomes an allegory for other people's problems, and that is fine. The irony lies in the fact that, however much we want to believe it, this notion of certainty simply isn't true. For the few extraordinary tales of survival that occasionally emerge, there are so many more terrible struggles of which we never hear because the participants did not survive to tell us.

More than once I have had to rely on the selfless courage and the skill of others to rescue me. My life has been saved on at least three occasions, and I owe debts of gratitude that cannot be repaid. All those involved took part not for payment or flattering gratitude but simply because that is how they naturally behaved, and how they expected others to behave towards them. It was a basic tenet of their education in the mountains that they should always go to the aid of those in difficulty. Criticism and condemnation can come afterwards, if deserved, but help always comes first. We all know this, and I believe that, depending on abilities, almost every climber would make some sort of effort to help. For mountain guides, agreement to this unwritten code – always to go to the aid of those in trouble – is like some sort of Hippocratic oath, an essential requirement for their qualification. Paradoxically, they can find themselves in a Catch-22 situation as a result. Guides who find it essential to give medication in order to rescue a victim safely may find themselves liable to prosecution in cases where only doctors are permitted to administer certain drugs. I have yet to meet a single guide who would do anything other than what he thought was right and damn the consequences of prosecution. Sometimes the law can be an ass.

Only a year ago I received a letter from a climber and lawyer in Australia who was putting together a book on the liability of landowners and managers of climbing areas for climbing accidents. Gordon Brysland was also interested in more general issues concerning responsibility for belaying, equipment failure, climbing gyms and the liability of schools, as well as a few criminal issues. It was on this last point that he wanted my opinion as to the intriguing legal position of Simon Yates after he had cut the rope connecting me to him in a desperate situation on Siula Grande. Brysland wondered whether Simon could have been indicted for murder. At first I laughed, but gradually it dawned on me that there were some very real reasons why it was possible. I giggled nervously as I read that *'had Joe died on Siula Grande, technically speaking, Simon could have been charged with murder and no defence of necessity would have saved him from conviction at the Old Bailey.'* Indeed the conclusion was that, although a murder prosecution could have been successful, in all probability policy factors would have mitigated against any case being brought to court. If I felt a bit odd about it all, it did make me wonder what Simon felt when he received the same enquiry from the Australian lawyer. I am sure he saw the funny side of *'killing is merely an acceleration of death and factors which produce a very trivial acceleration (like cutting the rope) will be ignored.'* It sounded to me about as daft as saying that death was simply a prolonged absence from everyone else. The legal positions of *'self defence'* and *'self-preferential killing of an unoffending innocent'* made quite startling reading, but in the end, after I had provided Gordon Brysland with more information, he felt confident of establishing that Simon could never have had the necessary *'intent'* to be convicted.

There were some odd things to learn about the responsibility of rescuers, and I was surprised to see that, in law, U.S. and Australian Rangers have no duty to rescue climbers. Even more astonishing, I learned that in Britain not even the Royal National Lifeboat Institution has a legal obligation to rescue mariners in distress. Yet, if the truth is that you are not legally required to help others who are in danger or distress, you know in your heart that you must do so. There is a world of difference between legal obligation and a sense of ethical duty. We really don't need the Ten Commandments to tell us not to steal and not to kill: instinctively we know this to be right. And you try to save others not out of some foolish notion of heroic sacrifice but simply because it is how you would want other people to behave towards you. It is a matter of common decency, good manners and empathy, however old fashioned that might sound.

I asked Brysland if one would be guilty of anything in law

if one sat by without giving any help to the Indian climber on the South Col, and his depressing reply was *'nothing'*. He agreed that it probably wouldn't make you feel too good inside, but only if somehow you contributed to the man's accident, or had some sort of statutory responsibilities, might you be liable. He quoted the *Modern Law Review* which observed that 'law reports contain some sickening examples of callous refusal to help, followed by immunity from tort liability'.

After the blizzard that tore into the summit slopes of Everest in May 1996, what happened on the north side was chillingly reminiscent of what took place among the Dutch and the Indians in 1992. For whatever reasons, several climbers on their northern summit bid after the fateful storm climbed straight past three dying men. There was no attempt to give aid or comfort, nor even to make eye contact with the hapless victims. Once again pragmatism was the given excuse for inhumanely callous behaviour. On hearing this I was overwhelmed with a sense that something had gone seriously wrong, something was happening that had little to do with the mountaineering I had been brought up to understand and love. Were we irrecoverably losing the essence of why we went to the mountains; indeed had we already lost it forever?

2

Killing Time

Overcrowding definitely contributed to the disaster that unfolded on Everest's upper slopes in May 1996. Jon Krakauer, who summited that day and survived the ensuing storm, reported that the climb was marked by long delays due to bottlenecks forming at such crucial points as the Hillary Step. Lack of communication also caused confusion over which Sherpas and guides would fix ropes on the ridge.

Krakauer was one of a group of eight climbers of mixed ability being guided by Rob Hall who had made a successful business – Adventure Consultants – out of taking clients to the top of the world's highest mountain. With them were two other guides and four Sherpas. Another large group of six clients, five Sherpas and three guides were climbing that day under the leadership of the American guide Scott Fischer. A Taiwanese climber and his three-man Sherpa team were also on the ridge.

At the Balcony, a level area at the start of the south-east ridge, Krakauer had to wait an hour for the rest of his group to catch up. Later he experienced long delays above the Balcony while guides and Sherpas fixed ropes on a series of large and awkward rock steps on the ridge itself. Beyond the South Summit he reported almost falling asleep and losing track of time as he sat in the snow and waited for nearly an hour at 28,700 feet for one of the three guides and two Sherpas sitting with him to fix ropes on the dangerously corniced section of ridge on and above the Hillary Step. The Sherpas refused to fix the ropes and at last Anatoli Boukreev, guiding for Scott Fischer, led off, fixing lines as he went.

The wind had begun to rise. Although the weather seemed clear, the climbers still hadn't noticed a gradual ominous change far below them. Boukreev, climbing without oxygen, was the first to reach the summit, followed by the guides Harris and Beidleman, and soon afterwards Krakauer. Whilst snapping some photographs on the summit, Krakauer noticed that the clear skies of the morning had changed. Clouds had crept in, hiding the smaller neighbouring peaks of Ama Dablam and Pumori. Since the latter is more than 7000 metres high, it was a significant and relatively fast weather development.

Although Krakauer spent only a short time on the summit, when he turned to leave he realised that the earlier delays had used up too much of his oxygen supply. Wasting two to three hours can be a recipe for disaster on a climb that is so dependent on the weather, oxygen supplies and available daylight. It was twenty minutes past one o'clock. Below, strung out along the ridge between him and his spare oxygen at the South Summit, were the rest of the three groups. At the top of the Hillary Step he had to wait again while a long queue of climbers had ascended the fixed rope that he wanted to descend. As the wind rose, clouds began to cover the summit ridge.

Some of Neal Beidleman's and Scott Fischer's summit photographs, published in the American *Climbing* magazine, clearly show the deteriorating conditions. Fischer took a shot of eighteen climbers bottle-necked at, or around, the Hillary Step in what appear to be relatively benign conditions, with blue skies beyond. Neal Beidleman's photograph of Boukreev climbing towards the Hillary Step, however, shows his trailing rope being blown in a great arc out over the Kangshung face and Everest's familiar snow plume billowing ominously from the summit just above him.

Normally climbers look up at the sky to read the signs of impending bad weather. Being above these signs, it is possible that they failed to look down and note the changing weather that had filled the depths beneath them. It may have been difficult to judge what the billowing mass of clouds below really signified – harmless afternoon cloud formations or the approach of a vicious storm. In one of Fischer's last shots, taken while looking down from the top of the Hillary Step, a line of climbers led by Beidleman can be seen descending the ridge enveloped in gloomy clouds. As night fell Krakauer and another of Rob Hall's clients, Martin Adams (a Texas businessman), both of whom had descended rapidly, reached the safety of Camp IV on the South Col just as the full fury of the storm swept across the upper reaches of the mountain.

The constant loss of time caused by slow-moving climbers can only be seen as a critical mistake on the part of the guides. Rob Hall had always insisted that the summit had to be reached no later than two o'clock. Scott Fischer was in general agreement with this timing. Yet, for some reason, both men broke their own rules. Possibly there was a degree of rivalry between the two guides. They knew that if the summit was reached any later, then there would be a very real danger of clients running out of oxygen or being overtaken by darkness before reaching the safety of Camp IV, or both.

We will never know what made them continue so late since both guides died. Summit fever, perhaps induced by a false sense of security created by the presence of so many people on the mountain, is one possibility. Success on the world's highest mountain was becoming so commonplace that a degree of complacency may have also set in. Could they have forgotten the seriousness of the risk they were taking? Hall had been so successful with earlier clients that maybe he and all those with him felt invulnerable, certain to succeed whatever the signs were to the contrary. That luck with the weather eventually ran out for Rob Hall is not so surprising since he had been on Everest more often than most. Simple probability dictates that the more times you put your head in the lion's mouth the more likely it is that one day he will close it.

Five of Hall's clients, however, came to their own conclusions. Believing that they could not reach the summit by one o'clock, Stuart Hutchison (a Canadian doctor), John Taske (an Australian doctor) and Lou Kasischke (an American lawyer), unhappy with the delays, chose to start their descent at mid-day. Having spent such an enormous amount of time, energy and money on their climb, it must have been a very difficult decision to reach, and, as it turned out, they and Frank Fischbeck were the only ones to have made the right choice. Fischbeck, a publisher based in Hong Kong and reputedly one of Hall's strongest clients, had turned back even earlier. The remaining clients continued because that was what everyone else was doing, and the guides did not advise otherwise.

Both Hall and Fischer knew the very high costs of mounting a second summit attempt and were keenly aware of how important client success was to their future business. Rob Hall was under pressure since he had failed to get any clients to the top on his previous Everest expedition, and Scott Fischer, on his first attempt at guiding on Everest with his company, Mountain Madness, would also have been keen to succeed. So it is possible that good business practice, profit and loss, may have influenced their decisions.

The two big groups became intermingled on the ridge. Scott Fisher, acting as sweep at the rear, was clearly not one hundred per cent fit that day and never caught up with the slower members of the groups to tell them to turn round. It might seem obvious that many of the climbers should have been turned round as soon as it became clear that the summit could not be reached before one o'clock, but that required foresight, not hindsight.

Perhaps at a very subtle and sub-conscious level all these seemingly innocuous errors combined to produce a tragedy. If there had been half the number attempting the climb, and consequently half as many delays, then it might just have been possible to get to the top and down again within the planned time-scale before the storm set in. It should be noted that this was a short and vicious storm that developed rapidly. There had been a minor squall the previous evening which had petered out by about seven o'clock. Such weather was common enough to be a calculated risk made acceptable only by sound judgement and good timing.

There is little margin for error in climbing the world's highest mountains, and human beings are always fallible. Guides are often perceived as infallible – a dangerous notion since they can be just as vulnerable as the rest of us. Hypoxia, hypothermia and cerebral oedemas do not defer to experience. Guides, we hope and trust, simply make fewer mistakes than the rest of us because they are more experienced. They also have no desire to see clients die, or to risk losing their own lives in saving them; mortality is a great incentive to being a safe guide. Yet, with our unreliable human nature, mistakes will always be made, and the consequences can be appalling. Simply being there is risky enough.

When Neal Beidleman left the summit with four clients at three o'clock there were as many as sixteen people between them and the distinctive hump of the South Summit. On his descent, with a storm visible lower down the mountain, he was to meet Scott Fischer on his way up between the South Summit and the Hillary Step. Fischer reached the summit at 3:30 p.m., behind the Taiwanese climber, Makalu Gau, and his two Sherpas. It is now clear that Fischer was already struggling, possibly with the beginnings of some serious altitude sickness, but in the general stupefaction of tiredness and hypoxia brought about by the climb, no one really noticed. He, after all, was the strong man, one of the head guides. There is some reason to believe that another guide, Andy Harris, was also deteriorating by the time he had descended to the South Summit. Later, writing in *Esquire* magazine, Krakauer stated that his friend's behaviour was oddly irrational, for he repeatedly claimed that all the oxygen bottles at the South Summit stash were empty when everyone knew that this was not the case. But Harris was supposed to be the infallible guide, and in his own state of hypoxic lethargy Krakauer failed to register the full extent of his friend's condition.

Rob Hall was the last to leave the summit. He had waited for his friend and client Doug Hansen, even going part way down the summit ridge to help him up. While descending from the summit, with his oxygen finished, Hansen collapsed above the Hillary Step. To judge by Krakauer's view of his friend's strange behaviour, Andy Harris may already have been suffering the insidious effects of cerebral oedema as he waited at the South Summit for Hall and Hansen to reach him.

He was last seen by Lobsang Jangbu, Scott Fischer's Sirdar, heading back up the summit ridge at five o'clock to help Hall and Hansen. Since all three men died, it is hard to know exactly what happened, but the consensus of opinion suggests that Doug Hansen fell from the summit ridge somewhere below the Hillary Step. It has been estimated that it took Hall and Harris, burdened as they were by the exhausted Hansen, close to twelve hours to make the descent from above the Hillary Step to the South Summit – a passage normally done in half an hour.

A garbled radio call intercepted by Guy Cotter, a close friend of the two guides, who was climbing on the neighbouring peak of Pumori at the time, suggests that they were still desperately trying to encourage Hansen to keep going at almost three in the morning. Thirteen days later, summit climbers from an IMAX team led by David Breashears, who were making a film about Everest, found what is presumed to be Hansen's axe lying on the ridge just below the Hillary Step. Lower down on the South Summit they discovered Rob Hall's body partially buried in snow in a hollow beneath a large rock. No sign of Harris was ever found, and it is assumed that he fell from the ridge while attempting to descend in the dark. A confusing radio call at 2:46 a.m. suggested that the three were still struggling to descend to the South Summit. Another call from Hall on the South Summit at 4:46 a.m. reported that Harris had left him some time in the night. Two axes, one identified as belonging to Harris, were found beside Hall's body.

Rob Hall survived the night and through the following day, occasionally making radio contact with base camp. He said he was shivering violently and could not walk, which was hardly surprising after spending the entire night exposed to a murderous windchill of minus 100° celcius. Exhausted, frostbitten, and enfeebled by the intense cold and the effects of two days above eight thousand metres, much of that time without oxygen, Hall was incapable of moving from his lonely eyrie on the South Summit.

Valiant rescue attempts the following day by Ang Dorje and Lhakpa Chhiri failed to reach Hall, owing to the high winds and intense cold. They left an oxygen cylinder and a thermos flask of hot liquid some 200 metres below where he lay. His radio calls became increasingly muddled as his friends at the base of the mountain implored him to try to descend alone. Early that morning, he was patched through to his wife, Jan Arnold, on a satellite telephone call to New Zealand. She had climbed Everest with him three years earlier and was now seven months pregnant with their first child. As a doctor and a mountaineer, she knew at once from the sound of his slurred voice and her own knowledge of the mountain that there was little hope for her husband.

Having struggled for hours to clear ice from his mask, Rob was at last able to start breathing the life-giving oxygen in two full bottles he had found at the site of his shelter. It revived him sufficiently to make him announce on a number of occasions that he was preparing to descend but each time he remained still. The weather was clear that morning but the high wind that had forced his rescuers back kept him pinned down until the mountain was again enveloped in cloud. He told his friend, Guy Cotter, in the afternoon that descent was impossible. With his badly frostbitten hands, he would be unable to cope with having to clip and unclip from the fixed ropes at the knotted sections. In one of his transmissions he referred to the fact that his fellow guide, Andy Harris, had been with him during the night but now seemed to have disappeared. At the time nobody knew what he meant. Harris's friend, Jon Krakauer, had been convinced that he had seen Harris reach the South Col and then disappear. Lobsang Jangbu, however, said that he had witnessed Harris climb *up* to lend support to Hall and Hansen and wasn't seen again. It later turned out the Krakauer had been mistaken. Hall's radio call confirms that Harris had selflessly remained behind to offer help despite his own poor health.

Rob Hall made one more call to his wife, Jan. Both of them knew the score, yet Rob tried to remain cheerful. 'Sleep well, my sweetheart. Please don't worry too much,' he said in his last call to her at 6:20 p.m. on the evening of 11 May. He switched off his radio and was never heard from again.

While Harris, Hansen and Hall struggled for their lives

near the summit, the rest of the groups were fighting to reach the safety of Camp IV. Anatoli Boukreev, with Scott Fischer's and Rob Hall's approval, had descended quickly to the South Col, out-pacing the rest of the climbers, aware that many of the slower ones would run out of oxygen before reaching Camp IV, and that he would then be best placed to re-supply them. Some have criticised Boukreev for not staying with his clients, suggesting that because he was not using oxygen he was feeling colder than the rest and needed to descend quickly to find shelter. Beidleman, who had assumed that Boukreev was going to take some clients with him (which he did not do) later pointed out that there was plenty of spare oxygen stashed further down the route.

Given Boukreev's incredible mountaineering record, his work fixing ropes on the route, his achievement as the first to reach the summit without bottled oxygen, his subsequent efforts to rescue Fischer the following day, and the fact that on the South Col that night he was the only one capable of going out repeatedly to rescue all of Fischer's surviving clients, it seems that his decision was justified. Seven days after the disaster Boukreev made an extraordinary solo dash up Lhotse, the world's fourth highest mountain, in a little over twenty-one hours. None of the other surviving guides and clients could have even contemplated such a feat of strength, skill and endurance after what they had just been through.

By nightfall on 10 May a raging blizzard had engulfed the mountain, and Hall and Harris were not the only ones fighting for their lives. Neal Beidleman had descended to the South Summit with four clients in tow by four o'clock when one of his clients, Sandy Hill Pittman, collapsed. She had made two previous attempts on the mountain (in 1993 and 1994) and had now climbed all the Seven Summits. As New York socialite and contributing editor of *Vogue* magazine, she had been inaccurately described in that magazine as a 'world-class mountaineer', despite the fact that her high mountain experience was limited almost entirely to guided trips. Charlotte Fox, perhaps the most experienced client on the mountain, with successful ascents of Gasherbrum II and Cho Oyo, administered an injection of dexamethasone to Sandy Pittman in the hope of improving her condition. This strong steroid can help to alleviate altitude sickness, but it is very much a last resort. When once more they started descending, Beidleman had to drag Pittman down by her harness, an exhausting process, until after about half an hour the drug took effect. She was then able to descend under her own power.

Also in Beidleman's group was Fox's boyfriend, Tim Madsen, a former ski-racer from Aspen, who had never climbed above 4500 metres but proved to be strong and durable, and Lene Gammelgaard, who had just become the first Danish woman to climb Everest. They continued their descent in worsening weather and very poor visibility. They had been on the move for more than seventeen hours, with little in the way of food and drink. The wind increased, and it began to snow heavily as they staggered down the south-east ridge towards the Balcony. Klev Schoening, one of Fischer's clients, had halted his descent to assist Lene Gammelgaard, whose oxygen had run out, when he came upon a struggling Yasuko Namba. Together the two of them helped her down for a while before pushing ahead to the bottom of the fixed ropes, concerned that they could no longer see Camp IV in the storm. Beidleman took over and attempted to drag the diminutive Namba down towards Camp IV which was less than half a mile away and only 200 metres lower.

By this time their oxygen was finished and conditions had deteriorated into a white-out blizzard. A total of eleven climbers were now stranded in nil visibility, overtaken by darkness in the freezing blizzard of a storm at eight thousand metres. Neal Beidleman, Yasuko Namba, Hill Pittman, Fox, Madsen, Schoening and Gammelgaard were joined by Mike Groom, who had been trying to rescue a virtually blind and hypothermic Beck Weathers, as well as two Sherpas from Fischer's team, Tashi Tshering and Nawang Dorje. Weathers had been waiting at the Balcony for Rob Hall's return since seven o'clock that morning, having abandoned his own summit bid. It seems extraordinary that he chose not to descend with Hall's four retreating clients, or later when Boukreev had climbed down to him on his way back to the Col.

The snow and screes of the South Col are treacherously featureless in poor visibility. On each side vast drops plunge down the Lhotse and Kangshung faces respectively. Beidleman and Groom led the group to the left, attempting to keep clear of the drop off towards the Lhotse face, but as the storm intensified and the wind made communications impossible, they found it increasingly hard to keep everyone together. With the screaming wind gusting around them, the exhausted and disorientated group staggered across the upper reaches of the Col, pushed and pulled with bewildering force. Eventually, sensing rather than seeing that he was close to an abyss, Beidleman decided to gather the group into a huddle and hope that the storm would shortly blow itself out, or that a temporary lull might enable them to see where the camp lay. They screamed and yelled encouragement into the wind, tried to massage warmth into their frozen limbs, and did all that they could to fight off the terrible effect of the icy wind in what had now become a fight for survival.

High above them, Hall, Hansen, Harris and Scott Fischer were losing their battle for life. Fischer had collapsed on the fixed ropes at 8300 metres, despite the efforts of his friend Lobsang to revive him. Lobsang had short-roped and dragged Fischer down the mountain, an incredible achievement for the much shorter man, some sixty-five pounds lighter than his friend. By now Scott Fischer was showing distinct signs of cerebral oedema and hypothermia – incoherence, exhaustion and deteriorating co-ordination. A ledge was cut for him to rest on, and he was soon joined by an exhausted and near comatose Makalu Gau, who had been helped down by three Sherpas. At ten o'clock that night the four Sherpas finally left them secured to the ledge and fought their way down to Camp IV.

On the Col the huddle of eleven climbers was tantalisingly close to a tongue of scree that led directly to Camp IV. They were only about four hundred yards from safety. As darkness and storm enveloped the mountain there were now more than twenty climbers, including the two leading guides, fighting for their lives.

In the meantime, Boukreev had been out searching the Col for hours until eventually returning to his tent at 9:30 p.m.

Stuart Hutchison, one of Hall's clients who had turned back, tried with Boukreev to rally help from the others at Camp IV, but no one was willing or capable of going out again into the storm.

By midnight the snowfall had eased off, but the wind continued unabated. Stars became visible in the night sky above the Col. The outlines of Lhotse and Everest could be discerned silhouetted by starlight. Klev Schoening became convinced that he had worked out in which direction the tents of Camp IV lay. He persuaded Beidleman that this was their only chance and tried to rouse the numbed survivors huddling in the snow to get up and head towards the tents.

Only a few had the strength to comply. Others simply couldn't act upon his shouted exhortations. It was clear that many were not capable of standing up, let alone walking. Beidleman made a last attempt to drag Yasuko Namba with him as he had done earlier after finding her slumped on the fixed ropes but she could not hold on to his arm and collapsed at his feet. Weakened to the point of exhaustion, he could no longer carry or drag her inert body across the Col. He had no choice but to continue without her in the direction which Klev Schoening, Lene Gammelaard, Mike Groom and two Sherpas had guessed the tents might be. It was their only chance of help.

After a nightmare struggle the small group finally reached the tents, guided in by Anatoli Boukreev's waving torch. He at once followed Beidleman's instructions and set out alone to find the five climbers abandoned at the huddle. No one else from the camp would risk or was capable of going with him. At first, the weather conditions were so bad that he could find nothing and had to return to the tents for further instructions.

At the huddle Sandy Pittman and Charlotte Fox were incapable of helping themselves, and Tim Madsen, although fit enough to reach the tents had selflessly decided to stay and look after the weaker members. At some point in the night Weathers had stood up, mumbling to himself before collapsing into unconsciousness a short distance from the huddle. After Beidleman had left her, Yasuko Namba became comatose and unresponsive.

At last, on his second attempt, Boukreev found the small group and managed to half-carry, half-drag Fox back to the tents, leaving behind a bottle of oxygen for Pittman, Madsen and the helpless Namba. Weathers was nowhere to be seen.

The oxygen revived Pittman and Madsen, but it had no effect on Namba, and they became convinced that she was dying. Eventually Boukreev returned and, with Madsen following under his own steam, half-carried and half-dragged Sandy Pitman back to the tents. It was a phenomenal feat of strength and endurance. He was too exhausted even to consider going back again for either of the two comatose climbers remaining on the Col. Whatever people may think of Boukreev's speedy descent, his actions that night undoubtedly saved at least three lives.

In the morning the survivors awoke to the realisation that seven of their companions, including the two leading guides, were still missing. Four Sherpas accompanied the Canadian doctor, Stuart Hutchison, who stood in for the exhausted guide Mike Groom, to search for the bodies of Namba and Weathers. To their horror, they found that both climbers were still breathing but barely alive. It was Hutchison's opinion as a doctor that the two climbers were too far gone to justify the immense effort required to save them. Namba's hands were bare, frozen solid, and, like Weathers, her face was caked in a thick carapace of ice. Weathers, lying twenty feet away, had lost his right glove and was mumbling incoherently. Hutchison was later quoted as saying that Beck Weathers had 'terrible frostbite and was as close to death as a person can be and still be breathing.' It was far too risky in the terrible circumstances to attempt a rescue, and there was little or nothing that could be done to alleviate their plight. Sadly the rescue team turned back towards the tents. Getting as many as possible safely evacuated down the mountain was their sole priority now.

That morning six Sherpas had set off to try to reach Scott Fischer and Makalu Gau who had spent the night on an excavated ledge a thousand feet above the Col. Two of the Sherpas continued above this bivouac in a brave attempt to reach Hall on the South Summit. Both men at the ledge appeared to be dead when the Sherpas found them, but oxygen and some vigorous massaging eventually brought Gau back to consciousness. Nothing could revive Fischer who, although still breathing, was deeply unconscious. It was all the four Sherpas could do to manhandle Gau down to Camp IV. Later Anatoli Boukreev climbed up to make another unsuccessful attempt to revive his friend but found that in the meantime he had died. He brought down Scott's camera and some personal effects to a memorial service at base camp.

All the other expeditions on the mountain, with the notable exception of the South Africans, had selflessly turned their attentions to the rescue of all the survivors. The South Africans were too tired to continue with their ascent plans, having arrived at the South Col the day before the disastrous summit bid. When Camp II requested that they might lend their radio to the rescuers and the survivors on the Col after communications were cut off due to battery failure, the leader, Ian Woodall, refused.

Later that afternoon two highly experienced Himalayan guides, Pete Athans and Todd Burleson, reached the South Col as part of the evacuation effort. Burleson was standing outside his tent at 4:30 p.m. that afternoon when he saw a figure stumbling towards him, one stick-like arm outstretched in front of him, the hand a useless deep-frozen claw. It was Beck Weathers. Somehow a spark of life had kept going inside his dying brain and something had triggered it into action ten hours after he had been left for dead. He had awoken as if from a dream to find himself in a nightmare. The sight of his bare frozen right hand galvanised him into action and, despite being blind in one eye and only able to focus a few feet with his other eye, he had struggled to his feet and stumbled into the gusting wind, guessing correctly that it was blowing from the direction of the camp. A few yards in the wrong direction and he would have plunged into the abyss down the Kangshung face.

Weathers and Makalu Gau were eventually evacuated on 13 May in one of the world's highest helicopter rescues carried out at 6100 metres by the Nepalese pilot Lt. Col. Madan K.C. At home Weathers had his right hand amputated just below the elbow and lost all the fingers and most of the thumb on his left hand as well as suffering such severe frost damage to his nose that cartilage from his ears was needed so as to reconstruct it. At the start of our Pumori expedition I saw a piteous photograph, presumably sent by Makalu Gau to the manager of the Thamel Hotel in Kathmandu, which showed him recovering in a Taiwanese hospital. He appeared to have lost all the fingers and thumbs of both hands which now ended in what looked like shiny plastic knuckles. In fact he lost his nose, toes, heels as well as all his fingers and thumbs. They had both paid a dreadful price but at least, by some miracle, they were alive. It could so easily have been worse.

The survivors were left to reflect on what might have been. The trauma of the experience must have made all of them question the value of what they had achieved. If the storm had swept in a few hours earlier, it could have wiped out eighteen or twenty climbers; a few hours later and no one would have been harmed. If the storm had been anything like the sudden hurricane that had blasted Alison Hargreaves and five other climbers off the summit slopes of K2 the previous August, then not a single climber would have stood any chance of surviving. It is a sobering fact to note that the K2 storm also seemed to approach unnoticed from below and was equally short lived.

In such situations there will always be criticisms, remonstrations about what should and should not have been done, guilt about leaving people to die, guilt about surviving. Beidleman, despite behaving with exceptional skill and nerve as a guide, was devastated by the death of Yasuko Namba; by the way she slipped from his arm as he had forged on to get help. Yet in truth it could have happened on any of the crowded assaults on the Everest summit in recent years, and some have even warned that it was inevitable.

What does shine through this desperate situation is the manner in which everyone behaved. They fought together to get themselves off the mountain. They and fellow climbers from other international teams – with one notable exception – all hurried to their aid from different camps on the mountain. Neal Beidleman, Anatoli Boukreev, and Mike Groom behaved in the highest traditions of the guides. Even though it may be argued that Hansen should have been turned back much earlier, it is honourable that both Hall and Harris refused to abandon their charge. Some pragmatists might argue that this led to the loss of three lives instead of one; moralists might retort that it was a feat of heroic sacrifice and great humanity, despite its futility.

As is so often the case, the Sherpas made extraordinary attempts to save those trapped high on the mountain and seem to have received little credit for their actions. Lobsang and three companions stayed with Fischer and Gau till past ten o'clock at night before seeking safety themselves at the distant Camp IV. The attempt to reach Rob Hall by Ang Dorje and Lhakpa Chhiri was brave to the point of foolhardiness. The revival and rescue of Makalu Gau was exceptional. People behaved extremely well in horrendous conditions. Whatever mistakes were made, whoever is blamed, whatever the re-criminations, it cannot be forgotten that once the storm had caught them the guides did their utmost to save their clients.

Unfortunately, such was not the case for three Indian climbers trapped in exactly the same storm on the north side of the mountain. On the Tibetan side it was an equally busy season, with more than 200 climbers and their Sherpa staff – in all fifteen expeditions – camped on the site of the Rongbuck glacier base camp. Of all these expeditions only three were attempting anything new and progressive. A Russian team succeeded in making an ascent of a new route up a steep gully, dubbed the 'Siberian Couloir', which rises to the east of the North Col.

Hans Kammerlander, an extraordinary Italian climber, was the only person to summit without oxygen on the north side and he chose to attempt a hair-raising ski descent – his tenth 8000-metre summit without oxygen. He made it halfway down. His ski descent was halted by a lack of snow cover and a band of seracs. This feat was only matched on the south side by the Swedish mountaineer Göran Kropp, who not only cycled all the way from Sweden to the mountain, but climbed it solo, without oxygen, at the second attempt on 23 May, and then set out to cycle all the way home again.

Kammerlander ended up competing with a Slovenian team on the north side to be the first to make such a ski descent. Davo Karnicar, who the previous year had made a complete ski descent of Annapurna, hoped to ski the line of the Great Couloir but was forced to abandon the attempt after sustaining severe frostbite to the fingers of his left hand. The Slovenians, led by Viki Groselj, attempted the line completed by Reinhold Messner during his three-day solo ascent without oxygen in 1981, which crosses the North Face to reach the Great Couloir. Before getting to the summit, however, they were forced to retreat from a high point of 8200 metres without attempting the ski descent.

The remaining twelve expeditions headed for the North Col and North-east Ridge route. Technically, this is a harder route than the South Col, but from a commercial point of view, both routes can be regarded as the *'voies normals'*, or standard routes of ascent, sometimes disparagingly referred to as the 'Yak Trails'.

It would appear that a degree of friendly (and sometimes not so friendly) rivalry had developed between the Indo-Tibetan Border Police (ITBP) expedition and a Japanese team to be first at the summit from the north side. Considering how many people have successfully climbed the mountain to date, it seems an idiotic reason to engage in such cut and thrust competitiveness. The 25-strong ITBP team was led by Mohindar Singh, and on 10 May four Indian climbers set out from their high camp at 8300 metres for a long day's summit push. They chose to leave at eight in the morning (Chinese time), some six hours later than normal – a decision bordering on incompetence. They gave themselves no hope of reaching the summit and returning to camp before dark.

It wasn't as if they were inexperienced. Samanla had first ascents of Rimo I (7385m) and Saser Kangri II (7518m) to his credit as well as success on the north-east ridge of Kangchenjunga, the third highest peak in the world. I cannot understand why he would have chosen to take such a risky decision.

Of the four only Harbhajan Singh showed a modicum of sense, turning back at the steep rock wall of the First Step

(8400 metres), at four o'clock in the afternoon when he realised that it was getting too late. By 3:30 p.m. on the south side the weather was worsening, with dense black cloud seen from base camp billowing up the Khumbu glacier as the wind rose to storm force. A fearsome plume streamed out from the summit ridge. Jon Tinker, who was leading clients on Mera Peak (6480 m) in the Hinku Valley, reported thunderous black sky in the mid-afternoon, as if night had come prematurely. Despite a Himalayan weather expert seeing signs in his satellite readings of an early arrival of the monsoon, indicating a north-western passage for the storm from the Bay of Bengal, climbers on Cho Oyo also saw bad weather coming in the opposite direction from Tibet. Whichever way the wind was blowing, it beggars belief that the three Indians on the north side would have been unaware of impending dangers, compounded by their late start. Yet they continued on their way to the summit, which was still nearly fifteen hundred feet above them.

By the time Harbhajan Singh had chosen to descend it would have been impossible for his colleagues to summit and get back to their tents before nightfall. Even so, they carried on climbing the difficult obstacle of the Second Step, a precipitous eighty-foot rock buttress, and eventually reported that they were on the summit at six o'clock in the evening in what we can only assume was a raging storm. In their last radio call, Dorje Morup and Tsewang Paljor said that their companion, Tsewang Samanla, a deeply religious man, had chosen to spend time on the summit to perform some religious rites while they started descending ahead of him. In fact they had mistaken a snowy bump almost five hundred feet below the summit for their goal. It was here on the following day that the Japanese and their Sherpas found prayer scarves and evidence of religious offerings. Beyond this point they reported seeing no evidence of footprints.

This again is evidence of a quite shocking degree of incompetence, unless of course hypoxia and hypothermia had already begun to take their lethal toll. There are many reports of climbers at very high altitude experiencing strange feelings of well being and calm, and a sense of detached un-reality. Rational thought becomes exceedingly slow in these circumstances, as if it were taking place in a drug haze. Perhaps the three Indians were all suffering the insidious effects of altitude. There were reports that two head-lamps could be seen slowly descending above the Second Step at about 8570 metres, but given the reported weather conditions, this seems strange.

That they should have died in such a manner was totally unnecessary. Their decisions made the mistakes on the south side that day look innocuous by comparison. Harbhajan Singh, whose decision to retreat saved his life, condemned them somewhat contemptuously as suffering from summit fever. Failing to find the summit only made their deaths seem all the more poignant and pointless. Their only consolation might have been that they died genuinely thinking that they had reached the summit of the highest mountain in the world – apparently something worth dying for.

If this was as far as the story went, then it would have been just another sad chapter in the increasingly sullied history of Everest climbs. But much worse was to follow. The next day two Japanese climbers with three Sherpas set off from their high camp on their own summit bid. They were part of a highly efficient and well organised expedition which employed full siege-style tactics with ropes fixed for almost the entire way up and a plentiful supply of fuel, food and oxygen. They had always planned to make their summit bid on 11 May. If the Indians had known this summit date, I wonder whether their hasty attempt the day before was prompted by a competitive urge to pip the Japanese at the post rather than sticking to sensible planning and sound mountaineering judgement.

The Japanese party left early in the morning, determined to reach the summit in time to get back to their high camp before dark. They estimated that the ascent would take no longer than ten hours. By eight o'clock in the morning they had reached their first big obstacle, the First Step, where they found, to their dismay, one of the Indian climbers slumped in the snow. It should have been no surprise since they must have known of the Indians' summit attempt and their failure to return the night before. The man was conscious, although clearly in a bad way, severely frostbitten and mumbling incoherently. The two Japanese climbers insisted on continuing with their summit bid. The Sherpas, who are all too often and easily bullied into acting against their wishes, went with them. No liquid, oxygen or food was offered. Five fit, well-equipped oxygen-breathing climbers just moved on past the stricken man.

One and a half hours later the Japanese came to the Second Step, and it took them more than an hour to scale the eighty-foot-high rock buttress as the metal caving ladder, draped down it by a Chinese expedition years before, had partly come away. This sort of climbing is an extreme and exhausting undertaking at 8650 metres. When at last they hauled themselves over the top of the rock wall they came upon the remaining two Indians, also slumped in the snow, some thirty feet from the edge of the step. One man was unconscious and close to death, while the other was conscious and crouched in the snow as if attempting to get up and climb. The Japanese did not speak to the Indians or examine them in any way. They carried on for another fifty metres before stopping for a brief rest and to change their oxygen bottles. They even took in a little food and liquid nourishment within sight of the dying Indians.

By 2:30 p.m., after a further three and a half hours' climbing, Hiroshi Hanada and Eisuke Shigekawa had fulfilled their dream – one they were prepared to stop at nothing to achieve. Helping others had no part in the dream into which they had bought.

They happily radioed news of their triumph to their team in base camp unaware of the storm of horrified protests that their behaviour induced. It was at first reported that the five climbers descended safely to their high camp, passing the now dead bodies of the two climbers at the Second Step and the comatose but living man at the First Step. Later the Japanese changed their story, claiming that at least one of the climbers above the Second Step was still alive, and that one of their staff, Pasang Kami Sherpa, who on that day had achieved his fourth ascent of the mountain, had helped the ailing Indian down the Second Step. Presumably the Sherpa then had to leave the Indian because he was unable to help him any further on his own. In all of this, one wonders why nothing had been done by the Indian team to mount some sort of rescue of their own.

Richard Cowper, a member of the British 1996 North Ridge Everest Expedition, organised by the commercial trekking and climbing company Himalayan Kingdoms, interviewed both the Japanese climbers immediately they reached base camp. Writing in the *Financial Times*, Cowper reported Eisuke Shigekawa as saying in response to being asked why they had done nothing: '. . . above eight thousand metres is not a place where people can afford morality'. This is a shocking reflection on some of today's big mountain climbing ethics. His partner, Hiroshi Hanada, apparently distressed, added in faltering English: 'They were Indian climbing members – we didn't know them.'

What sort of reasoning is that? I thought as I read Cowper's account. I was reminded of Ronald Naar's rationale for not going to help the dying Indian climber on the South Col in 1992, and my suspicion that they might have behaved differently if the stricken man had been Dutch. I wondered whether Ronald Naar has since stopped to think about how alive that Indian climber might have been once he had learned of the survival of people like Seaborn Beck Weathers and Makalu Gau.

The leader of a Norwegian expedition has been quoted as saying: 'Friendship, closeness to nature, building up a relationship with the mountain has gone. Now it is attack, in old fashioned siege style, and climbers have to reach the top at any price. People are even willing to walk over dead bodies to get to the top . . . I shall never come back.'

Brian Blessed, the former star of the BBC Television serial 'Z-cars', was making his third unsuccessful attempt to climb the mountain with Himalayan Kingdoms. He was reported in *The Times* to have been outraged by the behaviour of the Japanese and was quoted as saying in his usual theatrical manner: 'Everest stank of death . . . with climbers running around like headless chickens, desperate to reach the summit first. I was horrified that such a high mountain experienced the lowest common denominator in human behaviour.' It was an emotional response from a man unashamed to wear his heart on his sleeve, and to whom I had once suggested that he held the altitude record for over-acting. Yet there is some truth in what he said. He claimed that when the Japanese team held a victory party, he went into their tent, ripped down their national flag, threw it to the ground and pissed on it. If this is true, then good for him. Blessed made a grim prophecy that in ten or fifteen years tourists will be paying a fortune to be taken to the summit in pressurised suits on a funicular.

There are some cynics who might claim that paying tens of thousands of dollars to jumar up a rope, breathing enough oxygen to get to the moon and back, isn't so very different. Plans are already under way to construct an hotel on the site of the Rongbuk base camp on the north side. Why not build a pressurised, hurricane-proof dome on the South Col next?

The other expeditions at the base camp were outraged by the Japanese, who seemed unconcerned at all the fuss and immediately dispatched two more climbers and three Sherpas to the summit two days later. They climbed past the frozen body at the First Step and confirmed that it lay only one hundred metres above the high camp. The majority of climbers in the base camp were appalled by the behaviour, although a few – more pragmatic and hard-nosed than others – felt that it would have been impossible anyway to get the victims down without grave risk. For purely practical considerations, there was nothing to be done. I wonder how they would feel if they found themselves needing help in such circumstances?

It was probably hopeless to attempt rescuing the climbers at the Second Step, but even so, it appears that a single Sherpa managed to get one man down what in reality is the hardest section of the route. If the man at the First Step was in fact alive when the Japanese returned from the summit some eight to nine hours later, then it is unforgivable that they did absolutely nothing. That climber had survived a savage storm and a long night in an exposed position, yet he had still been strong enough when first found at eight in the morning to survive the entire day without liquid or oxygen.

Surely if the Japanese climbers had had the decency to abandon their ambitions and, with their three Sherpas, had worked together, they could have saved at least one life. Four people could have worked at reviving the man sufficiently to get him moving with their assistance just as three Sherpas did with Makalu Gau from a similar height on the south side on that same day. The fifth climber could have descended to the high camp to get some essential supplies: spare oxygen, a stove, some hot drinks. They could have radioed base camp to explain the situation and request that help be sent up from the lower camps. They could have *tried*. It would have been desperately hard work, and would not have been without risk, but it would have had a chance of success. They seem to have forgotten a certain moral duty. Frankly, I find it unimaginable that they possessed such a narrow-minded, almost insane obsession with the summit that they could find it in themselves to ignore a dying man.

The pragmatists overlook the very basic and, to me, obvious need for consideration of one's fellow human beings. Even if the victim will inevitably die, does that mean you should offer him absolutely nothing, not a drop of fluid, a comforting presence? How can anyone climb past a dying man and still think reaching the summit is worth anything?

Simon Lowe, the leader of the Himalayan Kingdoms expedition which was guiding Brian Blessed, held firmly to the view that the behaviour of the Japanese was altogether unacceptable. He later told me that, although it might well have been difficult, dangerous and probably impossible to rescue any of the Indians, an attempt should have been made at least with the lowest of the three stranded climbers. There was, he added, a distinct division of climbers into those 'moralists' who found the whole episode unforgivable and those 'pragmatists' who took the harder line and accepted it just as part and parcel of the risks of high altitude climbing.

Nine days after the tragedy the British mountaineer and guide Alan Hinkes reached the summit with Matt Dickinson, the television cameraman and producer, who was working on a Channel 4 documentary about Blessed's third attempt on the summit and was expected to provide the high altitude footage.

Dickinson's determined display of climbing was all the more impressive when you consider that he had almost no previous experience. He told me later that he had done no mountaineering in the Alps and hadn't even been to the top of Ben Nevis.

The day before their summit bid they had arrived at the site of their high camp and found an Austrian climber, Reinhard Wlasich, collapsed in his tent. He had been attempting an oxygenless ascent, and when forced back by strong winds – and no doubt mindful of the earlier deaths – he had tried to find some spare oxygen bottles that the Slovenians had told him were stashed somewhere on the Messner Great Couloir route. Unable to find the bottles, he chose to set off regardless on several determined attempts spread over four days. By the time Hinkes and Dickinson came upon him, he had succumbed to the lethal prolonged effects of high altitude. The man was in a coma, and they were unable to revive him. There was absolutely nothing they could do for him. They gave him oxygen, but he died at two in the morning on the day of their own summit attempt. He was accompanied by a helpless partner who, in desperation, had implored the two Englishmen for assistance, knowing that in reality there was nothing to be done. Indeed he had already been advised on Wlasich's condition by as many as ten people who had been at the high camp, all of whom had said that he was in an irreversible coma.

Hinkes denied later criticism that his ascent, as with the majority of his eight thousand metre successes, was lacking in style and originality and not in keeping with his obvious skills as a mountaineer. New routes on big mountains do not seem to concern him. He defended himself by stating that his role on Everest was to get footage for the television company. But it was also his third time on the mountain and another failure would have been hard to bear. For Alan Hinkes, it would seem that Everest was just the biggest tick on the hit list which would guarantee him fame and financial security. He is well on his way to becoming the first Briton to climb all fourteen of the 8000-metre peaks, having succeeded so far on eight and nursing ambitious plans to 'bag' the remaining six by the safest routes in the next two years. It would be an impressive achievement, even if it does appear to turn his climbing into little more than a business plan.

When I talked to Matt Dickinson about the position of the Indian climbers, he revealed to me information that goes some way towards excusing the behaviour of the Japanese. Dickinson was adamant that it would have been impossible for any sort of rescue to have been carried out successfully. The first body was situated on the North Ridge itself, above what Dickinson described as the most difficult terrain on the entire route. The line of climbing between the high camp and the First Step involved crossing the Yellow Band, a notorious area of very loose and dangerous rocks. He said that he had been alarmed while trying to climb them in the dark, and that they had still required considerable concentration when returning tired that afternoon. This area of angled shelving rocks, lying in chaotic disarray in a pattern that has often been described as resembling scattered roof tiles, was ground that – in Dickinson's opinion – would have prevented any sort of evacuation of an exhausted climber.

He said that, strangely enough, they found only one of the remaining two Indian climbers in the vicinity of the Second Step. Presumably high winds had blown the second body from the mountain. Or perhaps the Indian climber who was helped down the Second Step by one of the Japanese Sherpas, Pasang Kami, had tried to continue alone, despite failing strength, and had fallen to his death in the process.

Furthermore, Hinkes and Dickinson found shortly after setting off on their ascent that their supply of fluids had frozen solid. Consequently they threw away their useless bottles of once warm orange juice and continued through a fourteen-hour day without any water at all. The food they had would have been of little use to a stranded dehydrated climber. If this had also been the case with the Japanese, then surely there was nothing they could have done. Oxygen might have helped revive the man sufficiently to get him moving under his own power – as it did with Makalu Gau. Even if it appeared futile, I believe some token effort should have been made, partly for basic humanitarian reasons, and partly because you simply cannot know what humans are capable of surviving – as Beck Weathers and Makalu Gau proved.

Dickinson's inexperience as a mountaineer also means that he might not be best equipped to judge whether or not a rescue was possible. He was nevertheless critical of the callousness of simply climbing past victims without making any attempt to examine, comfort or communicate with them.

'If, hypothetically speaking, we had found ourselves in the same position as the Japanese,' he told me, 'we would have been desperate to do all that we could, which was, in truth, not much. Given that our liquid was frozen and we had minimal food, there was little we could do except maybe offer some company.'

'Well, that's a pretty big deal when you're dying,' I remarked.

'Oh sure, and we would have done so,' he replied. 'I'm not sure I would have wanted to continue with the climb, but maybe Al would have done. His great experience as a high altitude mountaineer has probably meant that he can be far more pragmatic about these things than I could.'

'So you reckon you couldn't have carried on with your summit attempt if you had been confronted with such a scene?' I asked, wanting to be clear on this point.

'Well, I suppose in a way we had already done as much with Reinhard Wlasich. We found him dying in his tent and still went on to climb the next day.'

'Yes, but it's not comparable, is it?' I persisted.

'No, it's not the same,' he replied. 'We knew he was in that state before we went up. We had been told by a whole load of people what was happening, and he wasn't alone. There was nothing that we could do except offer oxygen, which was a fairly futile gesture and we all knew it.'

When I put down the phone, I turned to look at a large framed black and white picture of Everest on my front room wall. I stared at it for a long time, marking off all the routes I recognised, recalling all the legends and myths of Himalayan heroes that had been created by these climbs, and suddenly it all seemed more than a little futile.

3

Profit and Loss

Recent events have led to some outspoken criticism of all climbing activities on Mount Everest. Commercial expeditions, while undoubtedly striving to be safe, responsible and ethically well-mannered, nevertheless attract more and more clients who are less than capable of climbing mountains this size. Numbers alone have been responsible not only for many more summit successes but also for a huge increase in the death rate. By the early 1980s fewer than fifty people had died on the mountain since attempts had begun sixty years before. By 1997, however, the number of deaths had reached 150, of which a shocking 50 were Sherpas. There are those, myself included, who find this more than a little distasteful. Most of the bodies are never recovered – either because they have been buried in avalanches or have disappeared under collapsing icefalls. Others lie exposed to the gaze of passing climbers because they died at heights where it is deemed impossible to move or bury them.

Before his untimely death on the mountain in the spring storm of 1996, Rob Hall was one of the most experienced of all high altitude guides. His company, Adventure Consultants, had an enviable record of success on Everest, which meant that he could charge the highest prices and be sure of a regular supply of clients keen to reach the top of the world's highest mountain. That spring, he was to make his fifth ascent of the mountain, by which time he had guided a total of 39 people to the summit. During thirty Himalayan expeditions he had bagged five 8000-metre peaks – Lhotse, K2, Makalu, Cho Oyo, and Everest – as well as climbing, in an astonishing seven months, the so called Seven Summits (the highest peaks on each of the seven continents – Europe, Asia, Africa, North America, South America, Australasia, and somewhat contentiously, Antarctica). He had also climbed five of the seven second highest continental summits – K2, Logan, Mt. Kenya, Ojos del Salado and Naga Pulu. He founded Adventure Consultants with his great friend Gary Ball, who was later to die tragically of pulmonary oedema on Dhaulagiri. Guiding on Everest became a lucrative flagship of their operations.

Not only was Hall a superb mountaineer, he had a flair for organising the complicated logistics necessary to get clients, Sherpa teams, food, fuel, fixed ropes and oxygen in place on the mountain at exactly the right time for a summit bid from the South Col. Given good weather and a midnight start, one can then expect to reach the summit after some ten to twelve hours of climbing, allowing another six hours for the descent to the tents of Camp IV on the South Col before nightfall. Each client carries two oxygen bottles and Sherpa staff carry one spare for each client.

In the spring of 1996 clients were paying as much as $65,000 for the privilege of joining Rob Hall's International Friendship Everest Expedition. Doug Hansen, an American postal worker, mortgaged himself to the hilt and burdened himself with two jobs in order to be able to pay for this, his second attempt with Hall, to climb the mountain.

Guiding on any big mountain (but especially Everest) requires considerable expertise, and not just as a climber. In the generally warmer spring season there is an ideal period when clearer weather conditions and lighter winds offer the best chance of a successful summit bid. Usually early in May the monsoon approaching from the Bay of Bengal has the effect of pushing the jet stream winds north into Tibet, and for a short period there is a lull between the blasting hurricane force of the winds and the heavy snowfall of the monsoon storms. This weather window is not guaranteed but is predictable enough for everything to be geared in advance towards making a summit attempt around the beginning of the second week in May. These seasonal weather patterns are well known, and as a result the Everest base camps in the spring of 1996 were bustling with some four hundred people in a record thirty expeditions, all planning their campaigns with a similar summit date in mind.

With so many expeditions on the mountain at the same time, debate became necessary if a potentially fatal traffic jam was to be avoided. Even so, the importance of this annual weather window in recent years has led to some astonishing overcrowding on the summit ridge. In the spring of 1993 some ninety climbers summited; in one day a record 40 people stood on top of the world.

There has been an explosion in the number of those successfully attempting the summit in the last decade. It took 26 years to achieve the first 90 successes; now as many have done it in one season. It is astonishing how quickly a myth becomes diminished. On 30 April 1985, 32 years after Tenzing and Hillary's first ascent, Dick Bass was the first to be guided to the summit; his was the 190th ascent. He went on to become the first man to climb all seven highest mountains on the seven continents. Since Bass got to the top of Everest that summit has been visited by an astonishing 742 climbers (551 of them for the first time). Of the total 932 (or 726 first time) ascents to date, only 83 have been accomplished without oxygen, and 19 of those were multiple ascents by the same individuals, mostly Sherpas. Ang Rita holds the record of ten ascents, all without oxygen. This dramatic rise in numbers led to predictions of disaster caused by climbing gridlock and an unexpected storm occurring at the same time. Unfortunately, in 1996, the forecasters were proved right.

In that fateful spring Rob Hall, the most experienced and respected of Everest guides, called a meeting and agreed with the leaders of the various international expeditions, both private and commercial, on their various summit dates. First to go on 10 May would be Hall's group of clients, Sherpas and guides, in all a party of fifteen. In the event, three of Hall's team turned back, ostensibly due to worries about the frequent delays, while the others went on to the summit.

One other client, Seaborn Beck Weathers, suffered from problems with his eyesight on reaching a level area at the junction with the south-east ridge known as the Balcony, about six hours climbing up from the South Col. Rob Hall advised him to remain where he was and not to attempt to descend alone. There he waited, becoming increasingly cold, for over ten hours before descending guide Mike Groom, with a struggling exhausted client, Yasuko Namba, found him and helped him down. It seems extraordinary that in all that time he had chosen not to move down with those climbers and their Sherpa escorts who had turned back from their summit bids, or later for that matter, with Anatoli Boukreev on his dash down to Camp IV.

Heading up from the Col that night was a second group of 14 climbers led by the charismatic American guide, Scott Fischer, a strong climber with ascents of K2, Lhotse, Broad Peak and Ama Dablam to his credit. His team consisted of the three guides, Scott Fischer, Neal Beidleman, and the phenomenally strong mountaineer from Kazakhstan, Anatoli Boukreev, who had previously climbed the mountain twice without oxygen. With the exception of Boukreev, all of the other guides that day elected to use oxygen, although some, like Mike Groom, had previously succeeded on Everest without it. The general perception was that, as well as effectively reducing the height by a thousand metres, bottled oxygen also had the effect of keeping the climber warmer, more alert and physically and mentally stronger – essential for the leadership and decision-making demanded of a guide.

Boukreev, however, argued that there was a serious danger in using gas. The climber becomes too dependent upon it, and in the event of it running out, or some malfunction occurring, the effect can be all the more devastating and debilitating than for a climber who has ascended gradually without it. Mental and physical deterioration is swifter and more marked when the gas is suddenly cut off. At the same time, it must be remembered that Boukreev was by no means the norm and his extraordinary twenty-year high altitude climbing record without oxygen is second to none. The majority of guides on Everest insist that if you are stronger and more clear-headed with the gas, then it is irresponsible for a guide not to use it.

Another American commercial team, two British teams and a Taiwanese expedition agreed at Rob Hall's meeting to keep clear of the summit area on 10 May. A notable exception to this spirit of co-operation was a South African team led by Ian Woodhall, who insisted, to Hall's fury, that they would make their summit bid whenever they chose, even on 10 May if it suited them. Although the South Africans did arrive at the South Col on 9 May, they were too exhausted to carry out this inconsiderate threat.

The Taiwanese climber Ming Ho Gau, who answered to the nickname of 'Makalu', failed to keep this promise and set off with his team on the night in question, accompanied by three Sherpas. Makalu Gau's reputation was already well known. During a practice for their Everest expedition, the Taiwanese had experienced a disastrous attempt on Mt. McKinley in Alaska, which would have been comical but for the death of one of their team. Of nine who reached the summit, seven were benighted on the descent, five had to be rescued, some severely frostbitten. One man died. The cheerful and ebullient Makalu Gau was reported to have been shouting 'Victory! Victory! We made the summit!' as if unaware that he was being rescued or that one of his comrades had died. He, with some of the survivors, had now turned up on Everest, much to the consternation of everyone else. On the morning of 9 May, the day before the tragic summit attempt, the first major accident of the season occurred when one of the Taiwanese climbers, Yu-Nan Chen, a steel worker from Taipei, slipped and fell eighty feet while stepping out of his tent to attend to a call of nature. He subsequently died of his injuries as he was being assisted down to Camp II. His leader, Makalu Gau, continued up the ropes to the South Col.

The South African team was the first from their nation to be granted a permit for Everest, and with the personal approval of Nelson Mandela and plenty of financial support, they should have got off to a flying start. However, under the leadership of a British ex-army officer, Ian Woodall, things soon began to get out of hand. Three or four experienced and talented climbers in his team soon became dissatisfied. Andy de Klerk was to tell his friend Jon Krakauer, a client and journalist on Rob Hall's team, that Woodall was a 'total control freak' in whom they were not prepared to entrust their lives. The four best climbers promptly left almost the moment the team arrived at base camp.

Both Fischer and Hall expressed misgivings about the risks these two apparently inexperienced teams posed both to themselves and everyone else who might have their own plans ruined and lives endangered in possible rescue attempts.

It later transpired that Ian Woodall had been less than honest about his climbing achievements. He had never reached a height of 8000 metres, as he had previously claimed. The remaining members of the team had little more than minor alpine climbing behind them. I had met Woodall six years earlier when I stood in for Mal Duff as a guide on Island (Imjatse) Peak after he had torn ligaments in his ankle. Woodall struck me then as one of those obstinate clients who always know best and who insist that they feel fine when clearly they are suffering. On the ascent, Woodall consistently refused to admit to feeling bad in a macho display that was completely lost on the rest of us. Gritting his teeth, and against our advice, he continued on to the summit. There he collapsed to his knees in an exhausted stupor and had to be helped down to the high camp at 19,000 feet, where he slumped into an alarming state of semi-consciousness. He reached base camp heavily supported by Chwang Sherpa, whereupon we learned that he had no recollection of reaching the summit. We were furious that Woodall had endangered the safety of his guides in a stubborn display of inept mountaineering. I could scarcely believe that in the intervening six years he had amassed enough experience to qualify as the leader of an Everest expedition, a task that with twenty years of extreme mountaineering I would feel anxious about and unqualified to undertake.

So two of the least competent expeditions on Everest in 1996 were not commercial groups but the national teams from Taiwan and South Africa, and this fact contradicts the common belief that guided climbers are the cause of all the problems on the popular eight-thousand-metre peaks. In addition, the three climbers from the Indo-Tibet Border Police (ITBP) Expedition who died on their summit attempt also made some very basic errors that competent and responsible mountaineers should not have made.

While commercial guided expeditions have led to many more people attempting Himalayan peaks, there is no logic in the knee-jerk reaction of those who say they have stolen our sport, hi-jacked it in the interests of profiteering. On the contrary, for business to flourish in the risky field of high altitude guiding, it is essential that expeditions are efficient, well organised and safe, and that they are dedicated to the notions of good environmental and mountaineering behaviour as well as successful summiting. Punters do not part with large sums of money in order to participate in the sort of incompetence displayed by the Taiwanese and the South Africans on the south side and the Indians on the north side in the spring of 1996. Yet there can be no doubt that the great increase in annual expeditions has opened the door to unbridled competitiveness. As a result, the performance of the best teams is often compromised, and lives are put in danger, by the incompetent ones. All the same, commercial enterprises do tend to pander to the egotistic ambitions of individuals who otherwise wouldn't dream of attempting such an ascent.

When you apply for a peak permit in Nepal or Tibet, no one seriously questions how much climbing you have done. If you have sufficient money, that is qualification enough. There are those good climbers, commercial or otherwise, who consequently resent wasting time, resources, and all the money and hard work put into their climb going to the aid of people who shouldn't be anywhere near the mountains. In 1996, peak fees generated nearly a million dollars for the Nepalese government. Add to that the income brought into the country by the climbers who need helicopter flights, fuel, food, lodging, porters, hotels and so on, as well as the considerable amount of free publicity for the country's tourist board, and it is easy to see how reluctant the Nepalese government would be to reform its policy on climbing. Over-crowding and all the attendant problems are as much the fault of the Nepalese Ministry of Tourism as they are of the climbers themselves. In a very poor country, where the tourist industry has been in a decline over the past four years, income of this nature cannot easily be ignored.

In the last decade there has been a remarkable change in climbers' perceptions of Everest. With the steady growth of guided expeditions, the best of them led by Rob Hall's highly successful company, more and more climbers from all walks of life, and with less and less ability and experience, have realised that the Himalayan range is no longer the exclusive domain of highly experienced mountaineers. If you can afford the fees of a good commercial outfit, there is a reasonable chance that a sufficiently fit and determined person with little or no experience can now reach the summit of Everest. Unfortunately, whatever one pays, the mountain remains a dangerous and risky business. The steadily increasing peak fees reflect the Nepalese government's recognition of the bonanza. In 1991 the fee for any size of team was $2,300. By 1996 it had escalated to $70,000 for a team of seven, with an extra $10,000 for every additional climber up to a limit of twelve. It certainly hasn't deterred the climbers, hence the sight of so many people camped on the chaotic rubble of the Khumbu glacier in the spring of 1996.

Air travel and mass tourism have seen to it that access to the world's highest mountains has never been easier. A Himalayan Easter holiday, including ascents of a couple of twenty-thousand-foot mountains, is no longer a pipe dream but one of the staple holidays advertised in almost every trekking brochure you open. Everest is simply another holiday destination, just more expensive than all the others, as befits its size. Everyone benefits, except of course the mountain.

'Real climbing', as Eric Shipton once referred to it, is now in danger of being sullied by the circus on Everest. As the world's highest peak, Everest should be a lofty symbol of only the highest and purest aspirations. If it is treated in the present manner, why not take that standard of climbing behaviour and apply it to every other mountain? If you join the hordes jumaring up Ama Dablam, you can see the way things have already gone.

After reaching the summit of Everest with Edmund Hillary in 1953, Sherpa Tenzing said that as he climbed he craved forgiveness for every step he cut into her side. To the Sherpas the mountain is the abode of the Gods, a place of reverence, not something to be conquered for the sake of personal glory and the embellishment of ego.

Erhard Loretan is one of the few leading mountaineers to suggest that the best way to stop the farcical situation on Everest from getting any worse would be to ban the use of oxygen altogether. This would have the immediate effect of reducing summiteers to only the few very competent and extremely fit world-class mountaineers capable of such a climb. The theory is that if the mountain were only climbed by the elite, employing fair means, then the circus days would be over.

It is now quite common practice for all the other eight-thousand-metre peaks to be climbed without oxygen. A notable recent exception was Ronald Naar's 1995 ascent of K2, using bottled oxygen and with high altitude porters, shortly before Alison Hargreaves successfully climbed the same peak without the support of either. She was killed by a sudden vicious wind-storm while descending.

Another British climber, Al Hinkes, reached the summit of K2 on the same day as Naar, and afterwards came in for some spiteful criticism from the Dutchman, despite the fact that Hinkes had already climbed seven of the fourteen 8000-metre peaks, all of them without oxygen. In at least one Dutch newspaper Naar dismissed Hargreaves as 'the climbing housewife', as if she were somehow incompetent, ignoring her achievement only weeks earlier when she had soloed Everest, unsupported and without oxygen, in stark contrast to his ascent of the mountain in 1992. In what seemed to me an illogical defence of his own performance on K2, Naar claimed that his oxygen apparatus was playing up, and that consequently it had been more of a hindrance than a help. Why on earth carry all that dead weight to the summit if it wasn't working? Or did his porters carry it for him?

It all suggests a certain inadequacy and petty jealousy in Naar's attitude, and does nothing to remove my suspicion that the dying Indian climber on the South Col of Everest was no more to him than an impediment. So important was the kudos of achieving that summit that he even publicly disputed whether Bart Vos – the first Dutchman to climb Mt. Everest eight years earlier – had actually reached the top. Vos is an impressive climber who has made solo ascents of not only Cho Oyo but also a new route on Dhaulagiri (at 8167m the seventh highest mountain in the world). When I met him in Holland last year, he struck me as a friendly, open and entirely honourable man for whom such ego squabbles are distasteful and irrelevant to the whole business of climbing.

After Alison Hargreaves had been accorded 'star' status for her Everest triumph, with banner front page headlines in the press, Al Hinkes joined her on K2 with members of an American team which employed neither high altitude porters nor oxygen. It was the second leg of her attempt to solo the world's three highest peaks in a year. Taking advantage of a brief spell of fine weather, Hinkes went with the Dutch team in a dash for the summit on 17 June while the Americans were still acclimatising. His triumphant return to base camp must have been a bitter pill for Alison to swallow after she had failed to persuade the Americans to seize the same opportunity. With the media spotlight on her, some people believe she may have felt pushed into making desperate and perhaps foolhardy attempts to reach the top of K2.

When Hargreaves and five of her companions were killed in the savage storm that engulfed the mountain on the evening of 13 August, it created considerable speculation about how she had died and why. The expedition liaison officer, Captain Fawad of the Pakistani army rescue services, said he had pleaded with her not to make a third attempt. 'It was suicidal and I told her so,' the press reported. One of her companions at Camp IV, Pepe Garcés, told reporters on his return, 'There was nothing wrong with Alison's judgement. One minute it was fine, the next it was very dangerous.'

Peter Hillary (the son of Sir Edmund Hillary), probably the most experienced climber on the mountain that day, had turned back from the summit attempt at noon, having seen ominous cloud build up to the north and south. Later one of his companions, Jeff Lakes, who had carried on, turned back before reaching the summit and began to battle his way down the mountain in the storm. Overtaken by avalanche, he managed to dig himself out and get down to Camp III, which he found had been destroyed by the wind. Lakes finally reached Camp II, dehydrated and exhausted but without any sign of frostbite. Hot drinks seemed to revive him, but he was found dead in his sleeping bag next morning. After reaching the summit, the rest of the group were quite simply blown away. If the storm had arrived a few hours later, the dead may have been celebrated as heroes and Hillary criticised for over-caution. That he survived may be due simply to luck. Chris Bonington defended Alison's decision to continue even though she may, with the others, have chosen to ignore some of the danger signals. It is something he acknowledged that all mountaineers, including himself, have done in the past. Sometimes you don't get away with it.

Having walked away from the tragedy, Peter Hillary then gave a number of press interviews from Skardu in which he rather tactlessly managed to suggest that Alison had made a fundamental mistake in a state of 'summit fever'. 'I saw Alison,' he told reporters eager for a story – any story – 'and she simply said "I'm going up." ... Alison was a brilliant climber but she had tremendous pressures on her and she became obsessed.' He placed no emphasis on the fact that all six of the remaining climbers, two from his team, chose to continue. The three Spanish climbers in the group were hardly novices with ascents of Nanga Parbat, Gasherbrum I and Everest to their credit. It seems to me highly unlikely that the entire group could have been susceptible to the obsessive exhortations of one ambitious climber such as Hargreaves, as Hillary seemed to imply. He could not possibly have known how terrible the winds were going to be. The fated climbers knew that late arrival on the summit was common, and that in the past others had successfully descended in the dark, sometimes in bad weather, to the safety of their high camp in four hours.

There had been no hint of 'summit fever' when, in 1994, she chose to retreat from her first solo Everest summit bid, turning back on the south-south-east ridge because of freezing

1. Sunset glow on the summit pyramid of Mount Everest. (Photo: Joe Simpson)

2. The two Japanese climbers, Hiroshi Hanada and Eisuki Shigekawa, who passed by three dying Indians in their summit bid on Everest in May 1996. (Photo: Richard Cowper)

3. Ronald Naar at Everest base camp, Tibet, 1982.

4. *Below*: Everest base camp on the south side. (Photo: Chris Watts)

5. *Right*: The Khumbu Icefall, Western Cwm, South Col and summit of Everest as seen from the slopes of Pumori in 1991. (Photo: Simpson)

6. Rubbish abandoned at the South Col, as well as a Sherpa who had died the previous year. (Photo:Karl Huyberechts, Everest 1989)

7. The South Col of Everest remained littered in 1992, the year Ronald Naar camped here. (Photo: Karl Huyberechts)

8. Advance base camp below the North Ridge on the Tibetan side of Everest in 1996. (Photo: Simon Lowe)

9. Alison Hargreaves descending after her successful solo and unsupported ascent of Everest in May 1995. (Photo: Leo Dickinson)

10. *Below*: Matt Dickinson and Al Hinkes at advance base camp after summiting on Everest in May 1996. (Photo: Simon Lowe)

11. Everest base camp in the Rongbuk Valley, Tibet, in 1996.
(Photo: Simon Lowe)

feet when less than five hundred metres from the top. 'How many men do you think would be able to do that?' Alison asked a friend of mine. When he asked her why she took the extra risks of soloing, she replied that she had to think of her children and considered it safer to go alone. 'If there is no one else to lean on, you *have* to get on with it, do the sensible thing and neglect nothing, because you know your life depends on it.' She had no illusions about what she was doing.

The Alison I had met at the Banff Mountain Film Festival in Canada was a dedicated, enormously talented and driven professional mountaineer – no different from many other ambitious athletes, except perhaps in her modesty and wry sense of humour. She could see the advantages of being a woman and a mother, and she chose to promote herself as such. Undoubtedly there were pressures from sponsors, but she showed no signs of being unable to cope. She never denied her ambitions, overriding which was her wish to make a living and secure her children's future with what she did best – climbing. And she went about it with great care, prudent planning, and high levels of fitness and skill. Style and ethics were fundamental to her mountaineering. She did not court fame just to boost her ego and in no way deserved the scorn poured on her performance by Al Hinkes.

If she was pleasantly surprised by the accolades and celebrity status that came with her solo ascent of Everest in May 1995, she would have been amazed by what was written about her after her death a few weeks later on K2. The press and media coverage of Alison Hargreaves' tragic end was enormous. At first, in the confusion of reports coming out of Pakistan, theories about what had actually killed Alison – avalanche, fall, or storm – were muddled and inaccurate. A few journalists chose to pontificate about her moral responsibilities as a mother to her children. There were reports that someone might be able to recover her body. Huge sums were offered by one newspaper for any personal effects, especially her diary, that might be recovered. This announcement was introduced with morally self-serving angst: 'Climber's husband attacks "Scavengers"'. While the majority of the press responded with sympathy and respect for the loss of such a talented person, the story was milked for sensational headlines: 'Doomed treks to summit of an icy grave' and 'A mother obsessed'.

It is ironic that Alison used the press skilfully to her advantage during her lifetime and would never know the legacy it left to her surviving family. I am sure that she would have been less than pleased with the exposure of her children to prying cameras in their time of grief and would have deplored the eagerness of her husband, Jim Ballard, to extract the maximum amount of media coverage. At one crowded press conference in Fort William, Ballard told how the previous night he had accepted that Alison really was dead and that he had told the children. The kids smiled for the cameras in a bewildered sort of way as their father read out one of Alison's last letters to them. I felt embarrassed to be watching it on television and wondered what Alison would have thought. She certainly wouldn't have been impressed by the way he was then late for her memorial service, arriving with her children ten minutes from the end.

We all know how the press feels the need to put its own spin on stories, to make them appeal to readers and so sell newspapers, but what has become of any ethical standards when a story can be stretched out of all proportion so that private grief becomes public entertainment. If it's all right to film the corpse of a man you have watched dying without giving him aid or comfort, why not take two small children on an arduous trek to see where their mother was killed so that they could be filmed receiving what amounted to grief counselling for their trauma on the way? The BBC certainly thought that appropriate material for a long documentary on Alison's children.

I have received phone calls from journalists who wanted my comments as a 'famous climbing survivor' after tragic mountain accidents and resented being treated as a useful source of comments that would give spurious authority to hazy reports. There have been a few interviews that I have given to journalists armed to the teeth with tape recorders and note pads which resulted in a piece a few days later stating things I simply never uttered.

One such incident involved a couple of British climbers celebrating their fifth wedding anniversary on a climbing holiday in the Canadian Rockies when disaster struck and they were killed. Luke and Eva Parker were also celebrating the fact that Eva was a few months pregnant, something no one else knew until after the tragedy when Luke's diaries revealed the happy secret. There couldn't have been a more delicious tabloid story, brimming with drama and overflowing with pathos and morbid voyeurism. A few poignant wedding photos, a heart-breaking quote from a grieving family and possibly a few grim corpse photos was all that would be needed. After all, when is the press ever interested in mountaineering stories that do not involve deaths? This one was perfect. A quote from a so called 'expert survivor' would give it just the right touch of authenticity. As soon as the journalist began his first question with 'You were once left to die alone in a crevasse, how does it . . .' I interrupted firmly, and politely, to say I had no opinion on the matter. 'Should someone be left to die like that? Do you . . .' I heard the man say as I replaced the receiver.

It appears that the couple had been descending from their climb when Luke had fallen into a crevasse. He had either hit the bottom or become jammed a short way down before Eva was able to do anything about preventing or holding the fall. The autopsy revealed that Luke had died instantly from his injuries. Eva, knowing it was impossible for her to raise such a dead weight single-handed, set off down the hazardous, crevassed glacier to reach the nearest mountain hut and radio for assistance. Before leaving, she untied from the rope and left it on the surface of the glacier as a marker so that the crevasse could be found by rescuers. After she had quit the glacier and was approaching the hut, she slipped on icy rocks and fell to her death very close to the path up to the hut. Her body was eventually found and a search revealed her dead husband lodged in the crevasse.

A blind man on a galloping donkey could tell you what the story was going to be. The angle would be to emphasise the fact that the woman had left her husband to die in the crevasse. The pathos of the pregnancy was an added boon.

There was even a suggestion in the questions I was asked that she might have cut the rope connecting them – and hence the interest in me. It was plain to me that there were no Machiavellian deeds to report, yet it became obvious that at least one journalist wanted to put a distasteful 'spin' on the story. Eva had done her very best to descend the mountain in a brave effort to get help. Even if Luke were still alive, there was nothing she could do alone for him. She didn't abandon him to die. She didn't cut the rope. The fact that she untied and left the rope on the surface was good mountaineering practice. There was no sinister story here, only a poignant and sad fatal accident that befell two mountain lovers and their unborn child.

I first heard Pam Caswell's harrowing story in a Radio 4 programme entitled 'Cause Célèbre'. Pam and her husband Steve were competent and experienced mountaineers, as was Pam's son Simon, who was on his third visit to the Alps. That summer they had chosen to climb the Aiguille de Bionnassay in the Mont Blanc region of the French Alps. Up until then they had been steadily ticking off the four-thousand-metre peaks in the Alps, and this traverse up the South Ridge on the French side and down into Italy by the classic East Ridge required competence and experience. Lying to the west of Mt. Blanc, the Aiguille de Bionnassay is a satellite peak of that mountain and is regarded as a serious test of Alpine mountaineering skills.

The Caswells were well equipped, but things didn't go smoothly on their climb. On the first night they were forced to bivouac on the glacier and were sensible enough not to stumble on dangerously in the dark. After reaching the Durier Hut the next day they were delayed for a while by bad weather. Eventually they arrived at the summit of the Bionnassay and, having completed the traverse of the mountain, descended the East Ridge, a beautiful, airy, knife-edge ribbon of snow that led down the Italian side of the mountain.

By four o'clock on Sunday afternoon – later in the day than they had planned because of the late start – they found themselves negotiating the broad snow-covered glacier where the sun had softened the snow bridges over the crevasses. They felt it safe enough to continue as there was an obvious broad path, described as a 'motorway' by Pam Caswell, and most of the crevasses were easy to detect and cross.

With Pam, the lightest, leading the way, testing the snow with her axe or ski-pole where the surface looked suspicious, they made good progress. Steve, the most experienced climber, took his correct place at the rear of the party. Suddenly, and without warning, a ten-foot circle of snow plunged away from beneath Pam's feet and she dropped into the abyss. Her son, either taken off guard or perhaps having too much slack rope between them, was unable to stop the fall. His axe ripped out and he found himself wrenched off his feet and dragged swiftly towards the hole that Pam had made. With the impetus and weight of two climbers Steve was pulled straight down after them, plunging almost a hundred feet into the icy depths. They finished up in a tangled mass at the base of a huge cavernous chamber, glistening with beautiful ice formations.

At first Pam thought she had broken her back; she couldn't move her legs. She had landed awkwardly, with her back twisted over her rucksack and her husband sprawled across her lower legs. Only when she managed to move Steve's weight off her did she realise that she was unhurt. Simon had hurt his leg in the fall and was suffering from a headache, but was otherwise unscathed. Steve had sustained a broken arm and was bleeding profusely from a laceration to his head. His most serious injury, however, was a bad open fracture in his leg that was bleeding heavily. He had also become tangled in his rope and was choking until Pam could free him.

Pam did her best to attend to Steve's injuries, bandaging his head, splinting his leg with ski poles, and trying un-successfully to staunch the bleeding. They wrapped up as best they could in duvets, cagoules and over-trousers and waited for rescue to arrive. Steve's condition gradually worsened until a combination of shock, cold and loss of blood eventu-ally killed him at about ten that night. Pam, who only the week before had discovered she was pregnant, had the ghastly task of breaking the news to Simon of Steve's death and her pregnancy in the chill dark bowels of a crevasse.

Towards morning, seeing that Simon was suffering from the cold, Pam removed Steve's cagoule and warm fleece jacket so that Simon could use them. As she herself said: 'It wasn't going to do Steve any good, so it was more important to try to keep Simon warm.' The curved walls of the crevasse consisted of damp snow, and water dripped from the roof far above them. It was easy to see why the snow bridge had collapsed. It was going to be a long wait.

Because they were descending the normal route on the Italian side of the mountain, they could reasonably hope to be found by climbers making an Alpine start somewhere between three and five o'clock on the Monday morning. At about that time, they started to use the six torch flashes and six whistle blasts of the international distress call, hoping to attract attention. No one came. As it grew lighter they realised that the weather had broken and it was snowing heavily.

Their immediate anxiety was that their tracks would be covered up, the entry hole filled in, and if the storm persisted for long enough, then no climbers would be attempting the route. Given that Alpine summer storms can last from a few hours to several days, it must have been a very frightening prospect. But at least they were sheltered and out of the wind, and Pam felt, with perhaps a little too much optimism, that they could sit it out for as long as a week. Lack of fluid, and a severe drop in temperature during a major storm would have finished them off much sooner than that.

Although resigned to a long wait, Simon's confidence and resolve began to break on the following day. It was now Tuesday, four days since they had set off up the mountain, and they had been in the crevasse for almost thirty-six hours. At four that morning, a face and torch beam appeared in the entry hole far above them. A group of Italian climbers had found them, and they at once set off to alert the rescue teams. Four hours later a helicopter hoisted them from the crevasse and flew them to hospital in Chamonix, where they were treated for hypothermia and shock. Pam suddenly found herself, with no money and little French, struggling to get the news back to Steve's parents. Unfortunately his father learned of the loss of his son on the six o'clock BBC news bulletin that night. Already the British media was heading out to Chamonix.

Once Simon had flown home with relatives who had gone out to Chamonix, Pam was left to deal with the press and the distressing business of getting Steve's body home, with all the bureaucratic formalities that entails. Grieving and a little bewildered, she could have done without an ignorant press corps besieging her with questions.

'They were trying to make me into some sort of hero, to blow up the situation,' she told me when, by chance, I met her later at a bookshop. 'I couldn't understand it . . . I was a normal person who had gone out climbing, and we had had this awful accident. Why were they making all this fuss about it? I had lost my husband, and that was the important thing.'

I could imagine how she felt: a confused mixture of relief at finding herself safe and alive, devastated to have been widowed, and confused and angry with a persistent press that insisted on burrowing away to fix the best 'spin' to the story.

'Everyone kept saying we had been climbing on Mont Blanc instead of the Aiguille du Bionnassay, and that really irritated me,' Pam said. 'I got the impression the press was trying to make out that because it was a woman with her son and her husband, then perhaps they were bumbling idiots, up there on a Sunday afternoon stroll, when in fact we were experienced mountaineers.'

Any chance for Pam to grieve alone in Chamonix and come to terms quietly with the loss of Steve in sight of the mountains they both loved was ruined by the press. Apart from implying that they were somehow incompetent, the newspapers started bidding in a scramble to buy the rights to her own personal story. 'I felt chased by them, and wanted to flee, when all I really wanted was to be alone out there and grieve.'

At the same time, some papers seemed to focus on the removal of Steve's clothing, and this became the essential 'spin'.

'It was as if they were saying I had stripped him naked, or something,' Pam told me. 'They were just not interested in the facts and the need to use his warm jacket. Simon's jacket wasn't as good as Steve's, so it made sense to use it because it was so wet in the crevasse – and none of the papers mentioned that.'

I can understand that reporters have a job to do, and that it is not always an easy task. But are there no ethical boundaries to what they pursue and how they pursue it? Is it reasonable to hi-jack someone's personal tragedy so thoughtlessly and turn it into something that clearly it never was? If it were not for the thrill of reading about thousand-foot death falls, bottomless crevasses and massive killer avalanches, would the newspapers ever bother to report a mountaineering story? And when they do so, the inaccuracies are often quite astonishing. It has often made me wonder whether they are just as imprecise when dealing with subjects I know nothing about and have to take it on trust that they are getting it right. Often it is when they attempt to draw conclusions about accidents, or begin moralising and pontificating about the sport, that they get things wrong.

Occasionally a member of parliament decides to utter a few sound bites to the press expressing outrage at the inordinate high cost of mountain rescue, and insisting that people should not be allowed to be so irresponsible with their lives.

The press feels obliged to follow up on this parliamentary intervention, despite it being a field in which they are equally ignorant. Of course the subject has the advantage that people plunging to their deaths make good copy. Journalists like to start with the drama of an accident and swiftly follow that with a treatise on risk taking, moral responsibility to rescuers and economic waste.

In fact mountain rescue teams are unpaid volunteers who choose to use their climbing skills to help others in the hills. They are against the idea of professional rescue teams on the grounds that there would not be enough paid members to provide a comprehensive search and rescue service and unpaid volunteers would be unwilling to make up the numbers by turning out at two in the morning to work alongside paid professionals. As it is, research has shown that there is no shortage of volunteers, particularly in popular areas, which indicates that climbers are more than willing to rescue their own.

Volunteers also provide invaluable help to both military and civilian emergency services during natural emergencies, or even in dealing with acts of terrorism (volunteer search and rescue teams were heavily involved in searches after the Pan Am Lockerbie bombing).

The R.A.F repeatedly states that rescue work provides excellent opportunities for live practice in extreme flying conditions, and these are essential for ensuring good military performance. Such sorties would be undertaken anyway as part of training. Rescues do cost substantial amounts (estimated to be about 1.4 million pounds in Scotland per year), but as they are regarded as crew training exercises, almost all the costs are met by the Ministry of Defence. The much vaunted financial waste incurred by mountain rescue operations is a spurious theory picked up by politicians and journalists alike who don't bother to look at the official figures available from the British Mountaineering Council.

A quarter of all the annual rescue call-outs have nothing to do with mountains or climbers. More often they concern motorists stranded in blizzards, accidents in unusual and inaccessible areas, or non-mountaineering medical emergencies such as heart attacks occurring too far away for the ambulance service.

The media has tended to emphasise the increasing number of accidents without regard to the fact that climbing is one of Britain's fastest growing sports. With more than five million climbers and hill walkers, it is the country's second largest participation activity. Better safety equipment, communications and rescue facilities have combined to reduce the risk. In fact, B.M.C. statistics reveal that fatal accidents are far more rare than is generally believed. In the period between 1964 and 1970 twenty per cent of mountaineering accidents in Britain were fatal. Today, despite the huge increase in numbers taking part, the fatality rate is as low as twelve per cent.

Annually, there tend to be more deaths as a result of swimming and riding accidents than there are among climbers, and even angling sees almost as many deaths, despite a million fewer participants. Unfortunately for the press, none of these sports seems to match climbing for high drama. I suppose a story about someone being flattened beneath a fat Thurberesque pony, or an angler being swept off to America while casting for pollock, doesn't make for such gripping copy. The perception that climbers die in horrifying falls from ice-sheathed crags is, however, quite unrealistic. Most deaths occur on easy non-technical ground, often as a result of an innocuous slip that rapidly spirals out of control.

Mountain rescue costs have been proved to be negligible. Two parliamentary select committee reports on the benefits of climbing and walking to the Highlands and Islands economy revealed that a staggering sum, estimated to be between 150 and 200 million pounds, was annually generated by the influx of climbing and walking tourism. The cost of mountain rescue is a pittance when set against the benefits of tourism, equipment manufacture, and related service industries which create the huge economic impact on these rural and mountainous areas. When compared to the £70 million generated by the fish farming industry, and £70 million created by forestry in the Highlands and Islands, MPs' complaints are put into a different perspective.

We have no need of codes by which to judge our ethical response to situations. We know intuitively which is the correct way to behave. In our hearts we know what works best for everyone. To 'love thy neighbour as thyself' is a precept that everyone understands and most communities follow. So what happens when we begin to grow careless, selfish, or wilfully ignore what we know to be natural and right? The society in which we exist becomes increasingly cynical and the lives we live dishonest, almost without us knowing it, until it is almost too late to reverse the trend.

I suppose we are all guilty of putting a 'spin' on things; always perceiving only what we want to see and telling others only what we want them to hear. Yet, if those who act in the public arena – journalists, politicians, lawyers – do not appear to be guardians of the truth, then surely sooner or later we will all cease loving our neighbours at all. Perhaps I am being idealistic, or a touch naïve. Maybe my approach to mountaineering also suffers from this fault. I can't say I'm ashamed of it. Perhaps it was hard for the press – let alone the rest of us – to take a balanced view of Alison Hargreaves' achievements and her tragic end. She happily manipulated the press to her advantage and was open and honest about doing so. If she was naïve, it was only in failing to recognise that once you have hold of the tiger's tail it can be very difficult to let go without being savaged. If the press went into a frenzy after her death, that was hardly surprising; it was a good story, fed by misinformation, a scarcity of facts and too many from the sidelines leaping on the bandwagon.

Scarcely a month after it had all died down I was due to set off with a group of friends to make an Alpine-style ascent of a new route on the South Face of Pumori, a beautiful 7000-metre mountain rising directly in front of the south side of Everest. As the leader of the trip, I was preoccupied with peak permits, flight bookings, grants and the search for sponsorship. After Alison Hargreaves and Ronald Naar I was beginning to wonder whether it was really worth going.

4

Huntsman's Leap

John and Tat were silhouetted against a bright sunlit sea as they walked away from us along the cliff edge. I watched them, lost in thought about the Pumori expedition. I wondered whether I would ever get everything organised in time. There were five months to go, and problems with our agent in Nepal were already ringing alarm bells in my head. The distant figures had dwindled to tiny specks when I glanced back at Bruce French who was peering into the alarming drop of Huntsman's Leap. A relaxing weekend climbing sea cliffs on the South Wales coast was about to become very stressful.

I crept tentatively towards the edge of the cliff and tried to lean out over the drop. Fear prevented me from getting too close, and consequently I couldn't examine the rock walls near the bed of the narrow zawn. The cliff I had chosen to look over formed one of the walls of Huntsman's Leap, a narrow chasm (or zawn) that cut back about 400 feet into the Pembrokeshire coastline. The containing walls fell 140 feet to a tide-washed beach, never more than 60 feet wide and narrowing as the walls reached out towards the open sea. A thin channel of calm water was visible, glimpsed between the almost pinched closed walls of the zawn.

It was a stunning piece of natural rock architecture and it held a strangely hypnotic fascination for me. I had heard that climbers either loved the place or were terrified of it, but once hooked on the drama of climbing in the Leap, many felt there was nowhere better to climb. Since I had never been into the zawn, and had only seen it a couple of times, it was hard to tell why I felt so drawn to the place, why I enjoyed the sensation of being sucked down into this grim rocky crevasse. I was scared and attracted by it at the same time – an exhilarating combination of emotions, the essence of climbing. It was inevitable that one day I would find myself deep inside this limestone gash, trying to get out.

From above, it was an intimidating place, enclosed, claustrophobic, and a potential trap, with no easy way out. It was a tidal zawn to the extent that the sea flooded almost all the enclosed beach, so there was both the climbing difficulty as well as the hazard of a time limit caused by the incoming tide. The sea was rarely rough in the narrow sheltered base of the Leap, although it was obvious from the debris thrown high on to the boulder slopes at the back of the zawn that sometimes it could be a seriously inhospitable place in which to become marooned.

The only escape from the bed of the zawn was by climbing up the vertical and overhanging walls, and the easiest grade given to these climbs was E2, an extreme undertaking. Unless, of course, you wanted to risk an extremely cold and tiring swim through the tidal rips coursing round the rocky coastline of either Bosherton or Stennis Head before a safe landing could be made. Consequently, it was usual to leave an abseil rope hanging in place after descending into the zawn just in case of being unable to climb out by one of the routes. A tiring but ultimately successful climb up the fixed abseil rope would at least provide a means of escape. I was painfully aware that we had neither a spare rope to leave in place for the abseil nor any knowledge of the conditions near the base of the zawn. If we wanted to attempt a route, we would have to abseil on our doubled climbing ropes and pull them down to use on the climb itself. This would leave us without a fixed rope up which to escape

I pulled back from the edge and glanced at the wooden signpost hammered into the grassy bank near the footpath. It warned climbers that the rocks were polluted with oil and that it was dangerous to attempt to climb in the Leap.

'How about it?' Bruce French asked as he peered into the chasm. 'It doesn't look so bad really.' Fear seemed to be absent from the character of this former England wicket keeper, accustomed as he was to being on the receiving end of West Indian fast bowling.

'You're kidding?' I said dubiously, dragging my eyes from the signpost. 'There was talk about the bottom forty feet being oiled, but I can't really make it out from here. They wouldn't put a notice up if it wasn't oiled, would they?'

'Well, I can see a dark line – there.' Bruce was pointing over my shoulder.

'Yeah, I saw that, but it could just as well be the tide mark as oil. You often get dark lichen or algae growth at that level.'

'Lichen in sea water?'

'Algae then, I don't know. Anyway, you know what I mean. It's impossible to tell from up here.'

'So we'd better have a closer look down there then,' Bruce said with a mischievous grin. 'We don't know how old that sign is anyway, and we've seen hardly any oil so far, despite all the scare stories. Come on, let's do it.'

I edged away from the clifftop until I could rise slowly to my feet. 'Why did I even think of doing this?' I complained quietly to myself. I peered hopefully to the west, in the direction of Crickmail Point, where John and Tat had headed, but there was no sign of them. They seemed determined to have nothing to do with climbing in Huntsman's Leap, for as soon as Bruce had come up with the idea, they had laughed derisively and carried on walking without once looking back. 'They're not fools,' I muttered as I turned to watch Bruce searching the clifftop for a suitable anchor point.

'We've only got our lead ropes,' I said. 'We don't have a spare abseil rope to leave in place. If we pull it down, we'll have no way out if it's heavily oiled,' I added plaintively. 'And I don't fancy the swim.' I looked at the sea framed by the narrow walls of the zawn. At this time of year (May Bank holiday) the sea would be at its coldest, having had the whole winter in which to cool. I doubted whether you could survive in such temperatures for long enough to make the swim out to the nearest landing.

'Okay, so we'll climb on a single rope then,' Bruce announced, instantly quashing my hope for a reprieve. 'We'll abseil on one, leave it in place, and lead on the other. If we get the correct abseil point it should hang directly in line with the route we want to take.

'Bloody Nora,' I muttered, feeling dejected. 'All right then, but you can lead it. There's no way I'm going to lead on a single rope.'

'Okay, no problem,' Bruce agreed, beaming happily. 'That means you abseil first as you might have to set up a hanging belay above any oil line you might find. Should be fun,' he added. 'Mind the ropes on the oil. Probably wouldn't do them any good.'

As I began to step gingerly over the edge of the cliff I glanced to my right down the length of the zawn to where it narrowed. I saw a glimmer of dark water heave beneath the boulder choke as a wave surged into the cramped entrance. From far below me came strange bellows of noise that echoed around the walls of the zawn. There was an eerie, tortured quality to the sound. I quickly searched the beach area, a chaotic jumble of water-rounded boulders, but couldn't see the source of the echoing noises. The tide was on the turn. It had been clear of the base of our route long enough for the lower walls to have dried off, even though thin slices of afternoon sun only ever reached the upper walls of the Leap. A breezy on-shore wind would have helped to drive off any remaining moisture. I shivered as I slid down into the shadows. The strange sounds had a rhythmic quality to them which I realised was due to the ebb and flood of the sea. Something jammed in the mouth of the zawn was lifting and falling among the half exposed boulders at the water's edge.

Twenty feet from the boulder beach I jammed the abseil rope tight and bounced out from the wall, trying to get a better view of the rock. I could see a distinct dark tide mark but it didn't appear to be slimy or show traces of the thick black crude oil I had been led to expect. The boulders and small exposed areas of sand seemed to be perfectly clean. Presumably the tides had washed the beach.

Three months earlier the news pictures on television had shown beaches around Milford Haven and the Pembrokeshire coast coated with thick blankets of viscous brown oil. A stricken oil tanker, the *Sea Empress*, had grounded on rocks no more than five miles from where I hung, and despite desperate and eventually successful efforts to re-float her, most of the vessel's fully laden cargo – some 80,000 gallons of oil – had spilled into the sea from her ruptured tanks. It had been widely proclaimed as one of the world's worst environmental disasters. It was one of the biggest oil spills off the British coast and in the top ten world-wide.

Predictions for the sea bird, fish, seal, dolphin, and shell fish populations were dire. Because a great deal was known about the ecology of the area from studies undertaken over the past thirty years, scientists felt confident that they could assess the real damage – how many birds had died, how the lower food chain (such as the sand eels and molluscs) had fared, and what this meant for all the other marine life dependent on them.

Usually such precise data about environmental pollution is not known, and in the case of the sinking of the oil tanker *Brae* on the rocky coast of Shetland a few years previously, early predictions were disastrous. Reporters stood braced against gale-force spray-lashed winds, talking of the stench of the oil and how it felt to breathe the air. There were grim hints that evacuation of both humans and livestock may be necessary. In the dramatic television footage the brown-slicked sea, surging and breaching over the tanker as it lay skewered on the rocks, told the story clearly enough, and then it was gone. Back broken by the ferocious power of the waves, the *Brae* simply disappeared from our screens as it sank beneath the winter storms of the Atlantic. The vessel not only sank but almost as quickly as it had become a sensational news item, it was forgotten.

A few months later hardly a trace of oil was left on the cliffs, the seas were clean, and the levels of toxins in marine life turned out to be far less than had been expected. Many people wondered what all the fuss had been about. How could the scientists and the environmental groups have got their predictions so wrong? Tens of thousands of birds had been expected to die, and when the oil sank to the sea bed, it was said that the entire food chain would be threatened. Even as I abseiled into Huntsman's Leap, there were still bans on all fishing in the area, both commercial as well as the sport of rod anglers, with threatened fines of up to £1,000 for transgressors.

I bounced gently on the end of the rope as the groaning echoed again around the walls of the zawn. It was an unnerving sound, suggesting that something terrible had taken place here. I hastily fixed several wired nuts in a flaky crack and arranged a hanging belay some twelve feet above the beach. A few tell-tale globules of light brown oil at the level of my feet persuaded me not to descend any further. I noticed with some irritation that oil had flecked the lower fifteen feet of my blue rope. Carefully, I hoisted it up and arranged it in neat coils across my belay slings. I shouted up to Bruce that it was safe to descend and heard my voice ring in decreasing echoes from the enclosing walls. A welcome shaft of sunlight just reached me if I leaned back on the slings.

There was a sudden screeching howl that made me lurch forward, almost dropping the neat coils back down the oiled rock. I looked frantically across the zawn for the source of the terrible noise, feeling my heart hammering in my chest. Far back, flung high up on a jumble of boulders at the high tide mark, lay strips of green corrugated metal which I instantly recognised as a container – yet it bore little resemblance to the large rectangular metal containers we see being hauled up and down Britain's motorways by articulated lorries. The metal had been torn into twenty-foot by five-foot strips as if it were paper, and reinforced corners and flanges had been peeled back as if flayed.

Looking towards the narrow seaward entrance of the zawn, I could just make out another large section of the container lying half-submerged amid the boulder choke at the neck of the zawn. While I watched, a slow heavy swell urged into the neck and the metal flap heaved ponderously upwards with a grievous agonised groan of scraping metal.

Bruce slid smoothly to a stop beside me.

'What on earth was that?' he asked.

'A container,' I replied, 'or rather, what's left of it.' I pointed to the green scrap deposited at the top of the beach.

'How the hell did it get there?' Bruce said in amazement.

'And how did it get torn to pieces like that?' I added. 'It must have been some storm.'

'Wouldn't you reckon that any storm waves would have run out of power by the time they got right in here.'

'That's what I figured,' I said. 'It certainly makes you think twice about getting trapped down here by a high tide on a stormy day.'

'Yeah, not much fun . . .' Another screech of tearing metal echoed round the walls.

'You know, seeing that ripped up container over there makes me wonder why there is all this drama over the *Sea Empress* disaster. What about all the ships that were sunk in the war – in both world wars, in fact.'

'So?'

'Well, there must have been millions of tons of shipping sent to the bottom, especially in the second war. Ammunition ships, troop carriers, cruisers, destroyers and God knows how many oil tankers. Where did it all go? You never hear about the horrific environmental destruction all that caused. I've never seen any accounts of decimated fish stocks or slaughtered bird colonies at that time, have you?'

'Can't say I have, but I wouldn't know,' Bruce said, organising his gear for the forthcoming lead.

'Well, I'm pretty certain no one got particularly excited about it. Admittedly they might have had more important things on their minds at the time, but after the war, while there was still rationing, when decimated fish stocks would have been noticed, there was no outcry, so presumably there was no such disaster. The sea dealt with it, cleaned it up and sorted it out.'

'What's that got to do with the *Sea Empress*?'

'It just made me wonder how serious this spill really was. All these doomsday forecasts, and the papers have a field day scaring the public about the calamity that has befallen us, and then it's all forgotten. The sea sorts itself out. It makes you suspect that you've just been hoodwinked.'

'Does it?' Bruce said dubiously. 'Don't forget all the work the volunteers and clean up people did. Tenby beach was awash with oil, but they cleaned it all up by hand.'

'Yeah, I suppose you're right,' I said reluctantly. 'And there are probably all sorts of explanations for the lack of war damage. Smaller tankers, a lot more oil was burned in explosions, and most were sunk out in the open seas, away from the coastlines. Out there the full force of the sea would break up the oil quickly, and in deep waters we would never know of the effects of oil coating the sea bed. It's not really comparable . . . but I get this uneasy feeling about what we're being told by the media these days.'

'Maybe it just wasn't an issue in the war. And anyway it's not as if the newspapers have any malicious agenda to follow. They make mistakes, like all of us . . .'

'Their agenda is to make money, and they do that by producing copy that will sell their papers. It makes you wonder who's telling the truth in the end, doesn't it?'

'How do you mean?'

'They went on and on about everything in Pembroke being ruined by the oil, and we get here and can see hardly any of it. How could they have got it so wrong?'

'Maybe we just can't see the damage. Perhaps it's under the sand, down on the sea bed, in the food chain . . .'

'Well. We've been climbing on relatively inaccessible cliffs where it would be hard for clean up teams to reach, and there's nothing to speak of here. Where did it all go?'

'Come on, you've got to admit the photos of it looked bad,' Bruce replied. 'With 80,000 tonnes of oil sloshing about the place, you'd expect the journalists to have *something* to say about it.'

'Perhaps, but we were all given the long term disaster scenario. That frightens people, sells more papers, makes more money.'

'You're kidding? They wouldn't distort that deliberately?'

'Why not? They are just like politicians who tell you only half the story and deliberately leave you with a slanted view. They say what they want you to hear and leave out the rest, which makes it damn difficult to show they are not telling the whole truth.'

'Let's forget about the politicians; no-one trusts them anyway. I don't believe the press hides or distorts things like that.'

'Well okay, not all do it, I agree. And yes, the tabloids do tend to be guiltier than the rest, but they all put a spin on some stories – and TV and radio do just the same. There's enough twisting of stories to make you think twice about what to believe. And anyway, you don't need many half-truths for people to stop trusting anything they say.'

'Yes, but that doesn't mean they spend all their time lying.'

'I didn't say they spent all their time *lying*. I'm saying that neither words nor pictures printed in the papers can be relied upon. They exaggerate, omit what doesn't fit their particular slant on a story, and they embellish each other's inaccurate reports. It's as good as lying if they know they're doing it. You're not going to tell me you think of newspapers as guardians of the truth, are you?'

'I'm not sure I care that much.' Bruce dusted chalk on to his hands ready to start climbing. 'But I wouldn't like to be without the press. Think what would really be hidden if we didn't have them?'

'Yes, but . . .'

'Look, are we going to do this climb or not?' Bruce interrupted me impatiently.

'Oh yes, sorry,' I said. 'What's this route called, by the way?'

'*The beast from the underworld,*' Bruce said, and there was another howl from the entrance of the zawn.

I laughed. 'At least it's appropriate. Hang on. Isn't there an easier route over there on the right? I thought that was called *The beast from the underworld?*'

'Oh yes, you're right. This one is called *Shape Up* and it's a bit easier. We can always try *The Beast* next,' Bruce said with his usual infectious enthusiasm.

'Let's just see if we can get up this one first,' I muttered as Bruce moved smoothly up a shallow groove in the wall above us. He climbed steadily towards an open corner and flake system arranging good and plentiful protection with small wired nuts and camming devices in the cracked wall. Every now and then he would shout down to say how good the climbing was, and his voice would echo around the cavernous walls arching above me. Within an hour we stood in the sun at the top of the crag, coiling our ropes and enthusing about climbing in the zawn.

'Shall we do another one?' Bruce said hopefully.

'Maybe, but, let's go and see what Tat and John are up to.'

I was glad to be getting some good rock climbing done. The steep limestone of Pembroke was not much good for the sort of mixed snow and ice climbing we would find on Pumori but it certainly helped boost one's confidence. My knee and ankle, injured on Siula Grande and Pachermo, felt strong for the first time in years, even if they did sometimes refuse to bend in the way I wanted. We walked across the grassy clifftops towards Crickmail Point. I had no fears about Huntsman's Leap any more and was looking forward to the next time we would abseil into its gaping maw. When, only a couple of weeks later, Bruce returned to the Leap with his wife Ellen, he was amazed to find that not only were all traces of oil gone, the boulder beach had been entirely covered by a smooth sheet of clean sand. Nothing remained of the shattered container. Even the large pieces on the high tide line had been sucked out by the colossal power of the sea and swept away.

The atmospheric rock amphitheatre of Mother Carey's Kitchen, for obvious reasons also known as 'Mother Scary's', contained the classic routes *Deep Space* and *Star Gate* on what is known as The Space Face. I had always wanted to climb *Deep Space*, the easiest line up the cliff but still an extreme undertaking. *Star Gate* was out of bounds to climbers between 1 March and 31 July, so as to protect nesting birds that favoured that particular spot. Climbers are happy to observe these restrictions not only for the sake of the birds but because, when approached, nesting birds tend to remain in their place until the very last moment and then fly off, squawking and vomiting half-digested fish with alarming accuracy.

After some hesitation, I allowed Bruce to persuade me to have a go at leading the first pitch. I struggled with the slimy salty rock, feeling ill at ease. The second pitch started from a free-hanging stance from which Bruce launched himself out and upwards, feet dangling in space above the dark cleft cutting into the cliff. I watched in trepidation as he hauled himself over the great roof and out of sight without any apparent worries about the giddying, lurching chasm above which we were hanging. Out to my right, the Atlantic ocean heaved gently up against the foot of the cliff, further adding to the drama of this magnificent and intimidating route. Once over the roof, the exposure and difficulty eased, and I listened to Bruce whooping his delight as he ran the rope out to the top of the cliff.

When it was my turn to follow, I reluctantly stripped the belay, painfully conscious of the yawning abyss and the echo of the surging tide crashing against the rock walls beneath my feet. The first moves over the roof required a confident and unimaginative approach of which I felt incapable. I was convinced that, if I fell off, I would swing out and dangle helplessly in space on the end of the rope. Bruce could do nothing to ease my progress by giving me a tight rope since it would pull me outwards rather than up. I spent a while on the precarious stance, holding on to the last belay sling and trying to summon the courage to make the first long, committing reaches to the left and over the roof. I was suddenly painfully aware of why it was called *Deep Space*.

It crossed my mind that I might be able to cheat. No one would see me if I attached a sling to the roof and surreptitiously pulled up on it. Bruce was out of sight and earshot and there was no one on the boulder beach below.

'Come on, Simpson, stop being a wimp,' I whispered to myself. It was weird to be scared and yet determined not to make it easy and safe for myself by cheating. I knew that in the end I would fall off rather than resort to aid-climbing tactics. Had I cheated, I would have known in my heart that I hadn't really climbed it at all, and I certainly couldn't bring myself to lie to Bruce, or anyone else, and pretend that I had free-climbed the route.

Eventually I took a deep breath and, with a loud squeak of fear, launched out over the roof, feeling my heart thump and conscious that I was breathing heavily. As always, once I had started, all my concentration was on completing the moves. The fear vanished, but not the shot of adrenaline it had produced. The sequence of airy and spectacular moves proved

86

to be much easier than I had expected, and soon I was climbing the sun-drenched wall above, having dragged myself out of the dark chasm below. Looking up, I could see Bruce leaning out over the wall, grinning as he belayed me. Out to my right, the Space Face fell in a great overhanging wall into the Atlantic far below. A surge of joy coursed through me, a mixture of adrenaline, relief and delight at the athletic nature of the climb.

As the sun sank into a flat calm Atlantic we sorted our equipment out and coiled our ropes. Tat and John strolled over from where their climb had finished at the top of Mother Carey's Kitchen. I watched enviously as they lit cigarettes and inhaled deeply. I had given up smoking two months earlier in the hope of getting fit for the Pumori expedition, and wanted to give it up for good.

'Hey, Joe,' Tat said, 'how are thing's going for the Pumori expedition. Have we got a grant?'

'Well, apart from a few problems with Arjun Gurung doing his best to rip us off all the time, things are okay. We've got a grant from the Foundation for Sports and Arts and the Mount Everest Foundation to cover you, me, Ric and Ray on the South Buttress, but Richard's team aren't eligible because they're not doing a new route.'

'Does that mean the cost has gone up again,' Bruce asked anxiously. 'Every time I ring Richard it seems to go up by another hundred pounds.'

'Now that you've decided to come it will be better,' I said. 'Richard tells me it should bring the costs down.'

'So,' Tat said brightly, 'How was *Deep Space*?'

'Brilliant,' Bruce said with a beaming grin.

'Bloody frightening,' I added, 'and I had a rest on the first pitch. It was really slimy,' I said lamely.

'Ah, well, there you are,' Tat said with a grin. 'Years of experience, you see. Makes you know when to cheat . . .'

'I didn't cheat,' I protested. 'Well, only a bit . . .' But my protests were drowned out by their laughter.

As a youngster, when I read my first climbing books, I had no understanding of the complex and varied styles and techniques that had developed over the years to enable climbers to get over whatever obstacles blocked their way. To me, climbing was simply a matter of getting to the top by whatever method made it possible. Style or the purity of an ascent meant nothing to me. Aid-climbing, Free-climbing, siege tactics, Alpine-style – these were terms whose meaning was only gradually revealed to me as I took up the long apprenticeship of my early climbing years. Rope work and knots, rock and ice climbing, crossing glaciers and crevasse rescue, moving together, safe belaying and leading on vertical or overhanging ground, self-rescue systems, route finding, bivouacking and prudent retreating were a few of the many things to be mastered. When to retreat and when to accept defeat and failure, however disappointing, were perhaps the hardest lessons to learn.

There were also the more mundane but just as vital skills of navigation, understanding the often lethal mysteries of mountain weather and avalanche conditions, assessing dangerous mountain areas, and basically looking after yourself in the hills. It all amounted to that indefinable thing – '*mountain sense*'. It was something you were not born with but it came with practice and experience over the years. It was a learning experience that would never cease. And it was not solely about practical skills because throughout the apprenticeship, served on British crags and Scottish winter ice, and eventually on the great routes in the Alps, a sense of history and tradition was taken in. Heroes of the past, whose ascents and styles made them the foremost climbers of their day, were associated with all aspects of the climbs I began to undertake. In short, I was swallowed up by the whole culture of Alpine climbing. Over the years an instinctive understanding grew of the best way to climb. As in ordinary life, the ethos of how to behave in the hills stemmed from a love of them.

I read Heinrich Harrer's *The White Spider* at the age of fourteen and was immediately hooked on this mesmerising story of that first ascent of the fearsome North Face of the Eiger. My hero of heroes was, and is still, Walter Bonatti. It wasn't just the greatness of his ascents, their boldness or desperate difficulty, but the style in which he approached them that articulated for me the passion that mountains can arouse in us. These people really existed; they lived, and climbed, attempted extraordinary feats, sought frightening, challenging exploits for no other reason, it appeared, than for the love of it.

At first, this seemed to me an absurd and senseless way to occupy one's time, especially if it also involved a very good chance of getting killed. These early mountaineers did not climb in order to win gold medals, or to become famous or wealthy. They wanted to climb the hardest routes on the biggest mountains in the purest way simply because it was a direct new challenge. Here was the ethos of the ancient Olympians, who taught us to value the act of participation above all else, even winning. It was a 'no losers' creed, a reflection of the respect and love that climbers held for the mountains. Nothing was done at all costs. The modern view of a silver medal for the fastest loser – a product of the money-fuelled competitions of today – did not apply. It was how one played the game, the style of one's success, that was fundamentally important to the early mountaineers.

Perhaps it appears romantic and old-fashioned today to speak in such terms when some aspects of climbing are more akin to warfare than to an aesthetically beautiful experience. Yet it seems to me that there has to be something more to this climbing business than simply deranged, flag-waving, nationalistic machismo if anyone is to enjoy the sort of numbing fear and frozen privations that mountains deal out at random. Self reliance, independence, a sense of freedom in a clean and beautiful environment – these are what keep alive a love for the mountains. At one time rescue was seen almost as something shameful. Difficulties had to be overcome by one's own efforts. Too often nowadays it seems that if you get a little tired, or sustain a minor but discomforting injury, all you need do is to get out your mobile phone and call up the rescue teams.

Maurice Herzog's brilliant account of the first ascent of an eight-thousand-metre peak in his book, *Annapurna*, was a revelation. Yet it was the Alps that most caught my attention – Comici's ascents of the vast overhanging limestone walls of the Dolomites, Herman Buhl on the Eiger and then his incredible solo ascent of Nanga Parbat, Gervasutti's classic pre-war climbs before his death in an abseiling accident, and Cassin's account of the first ascent of the Walker Spur on the North Face of the Grande Jorasses.

Over the years I unwittingly served my apprenticeship and learned the rules that marked out certain ethical boundaries. My fellow climbers taught me various techniques and styles, while I read in climbing magazines and books about such contentious issues as the conflict between Free- and Aid-climbing, between Sport-climbing and traditional climbing, whether to use chalk or allow bolts. I soon discovered that there was a difference between Aid-climbing and Free-climbing, and that the latter was subdivided into two distinct schools, Traditional and Sport-climbing. The Sport-climber would happily drill and fix bolts into a cliff face to provide reliable pre-placed protection while the traditionalist approach was to place all protection when actually leading a climb, and not to use bolts or pitons if at all possible. The traditional style was obviously a more risky proposition, and to climb the hardest routes in the traditional way would normally increase the risk of serious injury or death in the event of a fall.

The Sport-climber, on the other hand, armed with his electric drill, is quite happy to use bolts every three metres to protect him from a long fall. For him (or her), the joy of climbing lies in the gymnastic and almost dance-like quality of their movement on the rock. They don't want anything as intrusive as terror to spoil the moment, nor do they want to mess about with the tiring and fiddly business of trying to arrange protection with small wired wedges or camming devices laboriously placed in cracks. This intense concentration on technique, the endless practising and training, has been a fundamental reason why present climbing standards are so incredibly high. Twenty years ago it would have been inconceivable to imagine that present day routes could be climbed free, without relying on aid.

Each type of ascent has its own highly complex system of grading and classification of how climbs should and should not be done. To the non-climber it must seem madness that such passionate attention is paid to the finicky details of an ascent. If there is one overriding cardinal rule, it is that climbers should always strive to climb either in the same style as the first ascent or in a better style. So if someone has already aid-climbed a route, by hanging on to pitons and slings, then other climbers would aspire to reduce these points of aid until it can be done entirely free. It would then be regarded as a free route, and an ascent using aid would be regarded as a retrograde step. Similarly, if siege tactics had been employed to climb one of the great faces in the Himalayas, then future climbers would either try to reduce the amount of fixed rope or oxygen or, better still, attempt to make a pure Alpine-style ascent of the route.

This approach is undeniably elitist; only the very best can climb at the highest standards in the purest style. The rest of us must aspire to be like them, to reach their standards and, if possible, improve on them. As with any elite, only a very few succeed, and they do not remain the 'best' for very long before another younger, stronger, braver, more imaginative, more talented upstart comes along and pushes up the standard once more.

Rock climbing, for instance, has developed to a quite extraordinary degree and climbers today are succeeding on routes that only a decade ago would have been dismissed as impossible. The majority of participants are pure rock climbers with no desire to attempt to scale precarious icicles or monstrous killer mountains; the very idea seems absurd to them. Yet, as specialists within their own sport, they have raised standards to unheard of levels and refined the rules by which people climb to a fine art. Breaking these rules – and there is no one to stop you – can, and often does, set off ferocious storms of abuse and condemnation.

One aspect of climbing ethics rapidly became apparent to me. Lying, or cheating, was very soon seen through and exposed. There were always those who wanted to appear better than they were capable of being and who embellished their achievements a little, sometimes quite innocently in telling a good story, at other times with intent to deceive. Although latter cases were usually soon detected, I never really understood why people should want to cheat in this way (I claim no purity or perfection for myself) because such dishonesty so obviously cheats the perpetrator more than the listeners. The cheat never wins because he can never forget that he is not good enough to succeed by fair means. Not only has he cheated himself, but the lie is desperately hard to undo. Admission of guilt involves a loss of face, and more significantly a loss of trust.

Mountaineers are the same the world over. We have the same values, the same aspirations, and the same love of the hills. The code of climbing conduct is universal – or so I once thought.

5

Dangerous Places

As I down climbed I looked through my legs trying to make out where the bergschrund (a yawning partially covered crevasse) marked the bottom of the slope and the start of the glacier. I could just make out the red and black shape of my climbing partner, Tom Richardson, hunched against the driving snow. It was still early morning and the flat light and blizzard conditions made visibility very poor.

'What do you think?' Tom shouted as I jumped across the bergschrund and stumbled towards him through the drifting snow.

'It's too dangerous,' I said. 'This lower couloir looks dodgy, so God knows what it will be like on the ridge. Do you want to have a look?'

'No thanks,' Tom said with a grin. 'I thought as much before you set off. Well, that's the end of our climbing. Come on, let's get back to the tent.' He stood up and turned to tramp down the glacier, careful to follow our drifted tracks from the approach.

We had been in Nepal for a month, having come out early to climb in the Annapurna Sanctuary ahead of our main expedition to Pumori in mid-October. With peak permits for Singu Chulu, also known as Fluted Peak (6500 metres) and Tharpu Chulu (5500 metres), we wanted to make an ascent of the entire south ridge which connected the two. It was a long, committing route and rarely climbed.

We intended making a pure Alpine-style ascent of the ridge in a continuous two-man push carrying all our supplies of food, fuel and shelter and without resorting to fixed ropes.

After establishing a high camp at 5000-metres we had made a foray on to the glacier to test out the conditions. Our plan was to wait for a settled spell of weather before setting out to climb the south ridge of Tharpu Chulu, and then descend its north ridge to pick up a cache of food and fuel, before continuing up the south ridge of Singu Chulu in a five day round trip. The entire ridge system was more than two miles long and involved a height gain of 1500 metres, which made it a serious undertaking. There was time for only one attempt, and the prolonged bad weather ruined our plans.

When we reached the base of the couloir that led up towards the summit ridge I climbed up about thirty metres in a blizzard of falling snow and gusting wind. Most of our previous tracks had been erased. I was uneasy about the conditions and decided to dig an avalanche pit to assess the risk. As I pressed my boot against the upper edge of the pit a great slab of snow peeled off in a single three-foot layer and fell into the pit. Under the exposed slab was a layer of unstable ball-bearing type snow. I climbed down towards Tom as fast as I could. Higher up on the exposed knife-edged south ridge of Singu Chulu conditions would have been much worse and a retreat was inevitable.

As we trekked out of the Sanctuary and headed for Pokhara and the flight back to Kathmandu we learned that the monsoon had been the heaviest and most prolonged for more than forty years. We spent a few days relaxing in the capital while waiting for Richard Haszko to arrive from England. I awoke early one morning to visit Pashupatinath near Bodnath. The most famous Hindu temple in Nepal was teeming with tourists and pilgrims alike. Smoke drifted up from funeral pyres on the far banks of the Bagmati river, and I could see the attendants stirring at the embers and hot ashes with long wooden poles. The river was in flood and a scattering of orange flowers drifted quickly downstream.

'Special yoga,' the Sadhu said as he reached to pull at my sleeve. I jerked backwards. 'Come see, only fifty rupees.'

I looked to my left where he pointed to a group of tourists standing beside a small shrine. Below me I could hear the babble of voices and the distant hum of traffic.

'Come, sir,' the Sadhu repeated, pulling at my arm. 'Good yoga. Special yoga.'

I was propelled from the stone staircase into the small square in which the shrine stood. A young Israeli couple looked at me and smiled uncertainly. The Sadhu held out his hand and I passed him a fifty rupee note.

'Whatever it is, it had better be good,' I heard an American voice drawl from behind me. Deciding he was not going to get any more spectators, the Sadhu walked towards a large pile of rocks. He turned to face our small group, pulled the orange sarong he was wearing to one side and tucked it behind his waist. Then he squatted in a semi-crouch, his genitals hanging free. There was a sharp intake of breath behind me as a middle-aged woman next to me covered her mouth with her hand without taking her eyes from the Sadhu's exposure. The Israeli girl looked bemused and asked me what was happening. I shrugged and pretended not to know.

A set of iron tongs about a foot long were produced from the Sadhu's waistband as he unceremoniously grabbed his penis, pulled it away from his body and snapped the tongs across it. It was my turn to inhale sharply. He then proceeded to twist the tightly clamped tongs in a circular fashion so that his penis began to spiral as if someone were wringing a piece of cloth. I crossed my legs and looked away.

The Israeli girl's hand shot up to cover her mouth. Her boyfriend took an involuntary step backwards and swore in Hebrew. A series of flashes flickered in the mid-morning sunlight as people took photographs. The middle-aged woman gaped at the spectacle, her camera hanging forgotten around her neck.

Having demonstrated the suppleness and strength of his organ, and his disdain for agonising pain, the Sadhu discarded the tongs and turned his attention to the pile of rocks at his feet. He laid a rectangular pink cloth on the ground and then carefully picked up a large chunk of sandstone and placed it in the centre of the cloth. A square grey-coloured block was balanced on top, followed by another lump of sandstone. The corners of pink cloth were knotted together above the rocks so as to form a sling, and the Sadhu made elaborate and theatrical displays to show how heavy each rock weighed and invited a member of the audience to try lifting the rocks. The man struggled to raise the precariously balanced parcel of rocks more than a few inches from the ground before the topmost stone tumbled out from the sling, hitting him painfully on his flip-flopped foot. A ripple of laughter relieved the tension in the watching group as the volunteer hobbled back to his place. I guessed the rocks probably weighed about fifty pounds.

Without further preamble, the Sadhu then grasped the knotted end of cloth, slipped it over his penis, which he grasped tightly in the fist of his right hand, and, straightening his legs, he stood up lifting the three rocks clear of the ground. The Israeli boyfriend and I groaned. A second later, as the rocks thumped to the ground, I was surprised to hear the Sadhu shouting in a remarkably deep and angry voice.

'Now. Take picture. Take photo, quick!' He gestured impatiently at me and the Israeli.

I glanced around to see the rest of the group peering through the lenses of their cameras. Feeling a bit uncomfortable about the subject matter, I set my compact camera to continuous and aimed it at the Sadhu, who once again was preparing to lift the rocks. With a grimace on his face, he lifted the rocks clear of the ground once more, and I pressed the button. Four or five frames rapidly clicked off.

The group dispersed, all talking animatedly as if they had been released from holding their breath. The Israeli man stood rooted to the spot, both hands protectively covering his crotch, staring incredulously at the Sadhu. His girlfriend looked stunned. I don't think it was the sort of Yoga they had been expecting. The Sadhu re-adjusted his sarong, picked up his tongs, rolled the rocks off his cloth, and disappeared into the shrine, some four hundred rupees better off.

'Jesus wept!' I muttered to myself as I turned to leave. 'And I thought I had work worries.'

I walked quickly down the stairs towards the burning ghats, careful to keep my distance from the monkeys that fixed me with greedy, beady stares. I passed two Sadhus who had already fleeced me of fifty rupees for allowing me to take their photographs. They were dressed in yellow and orange, and their foreheads were painted with distinct vertical stripes of yellow, white and red paste. A small iron trident lay on the wall where they were sat. The elder man had dread-locked hair that hung below his feet in matted tresses and must have been nearly six feet long. The younger man held up his hand, palm outwards, fingers splayed, in a salute as I framed the picture. I wondered how long it had taken his friend to grow his hair that long. The temple of Pashupatinath is devoted to Shiva, as well as being another name for the god, and the trident, or *trisul*, is his weapon. He is believed to live in the Himalayas, to smoke a lot of hashish and to wear a garland of serpents on his head. Judging by their appearance, the two Sadhus seemed to have done him proud. They smiled as I passed them and then quickly turned their attentions to a group of Japanese tourists who readily handed over their fifty rupee notes. I felt less guilty about taking their photographs. They should get stoned out of their brains on the day's profits, I thought, as I headed towards the golden-roofed pagoda.

At times I am astonished by how insensitive and intrusive we can be in our photography, as if we had some moral right to do whatever we like simply because we own a camera. I remember seeing a picture in a guidebook of three tourists taking photographs while they stood less than ten feet from a group of bathing women who were desperately attempting to preserve their dignity. The women were taking part in the *Teej*, a special Shivarati festival held in August for Nepalese Hindu women who are expected to fast all day and then bathe in the holy water of the Bagmati. It is possible to go unobtrusively and observe this ritual as thousands of women in brightly coloured saris come down to the river to wash everything three hundred and sixty times, singing and making their obeisance to Shiva and his wife, Parvati. They believe that attending this festival will ensure their happiness, a long life, and that they will not lose their children. The married women have red marks on the foreheads, and red – the symbol of joy and happiness and the colour for marriage ceremonies – is predominant in their saris. The three tourists were openly trying to photograph the semi-naked ladies as they bathed and prayed without the slightest concern for their feelings.

Most Westerners would be shocked if someone did the same to them, yet once they are looking through the camera lens far from home, any sense of decency seems to evaporate. I have often wondered how much this is derived from the example set by the professional photographers, the so called *paparazzi*, who supply us with so much lurid copy for the tabloid newspapers.

Phrases such as *'the camera never lies'* and *'the public has a right to know'* have been trotted out so often by newspaper editors as a facile excuse for intrusive journalism that perhaps we have become inured to the offence. Of course there are also talented photo-journalists whose integrity and professionalism are beyond reproach, but there can be no denying that many press pictures display nothing more than petty spite and puerile voyeurism. The orange peel cellulite on a princess's thighs do nothing for the interests of the public good and defend no honourable history of democracy and freedom. There is a sinister purpose behind the myth of the camera. If the camera never lies, then the photo editor does.

The media have been remarkably successful in persuading us that the camera is the defender of justice and the standard bearer for human rights. Yet careful cropping and shot selection ensure that images, both moving and still, do often tell a completely different story from that of the context in which they were taken. The camera is simply a tool; how it is used and for what ends are important issues, for where making money is the predominant motive, the first things to be forgotten are good manners, consideration and respect, followed shortly afterwards by integrity and truth.

Even the law unwittingly protects the cameraman. He can be charged with trespass for standing in your garden and taking your photograph, but you cannot demand the film with which he has stolen your privacy. By law it is his property. If the photographer stands in the street, then legally you have no rights at all. Telephoto lenses can capture perfect images from great distances, and tiny video cameras can secretly film at will. Yet there seems to be little moral or legal constraint on how these powerful tools are used.

A good humoured shot of a snoring politician on the front page of a newspaper seems no more than affectionate. A photograph of a smiling man adjacent to the story of his wife's mysterious death can be misconstrued when the reader is unaware that the picture was taken months ago. Making a perfectly ordinary person look dumb or weird is simplicity itself; the shock of being ambushed by a cameraman would make anyone look strange. If that shot is then used in conjunction with a dubious story about a pending court case or suspicion of strange sexual tendencies, you can bet that readers will jump to the wrong conclusion. No permission asked and not a law to defend them.

It comes as no surprise to read that one chief photographer of a widely respected newspaper said that if he witnessed members of the royal family involved in a serious car crash, he would take pictures first and help afterwards. Why bother with helping? An exclusive photograph of a princess's dying moments would be worth a fortune, especially if her children are involved. And of course it would all be in our 'interests', and for 'the public good', and oddly enough we would find it very hard not to look at such pictures. We are curious by nature.

Photographs are increasingly a common part of our culture. Anyone can go out and buy a sophisticated camera or a video recorder at no vast expense. If we have become as hardened to the notions of public taste, decency and privacy as our professional counterparts, then we will see no reason for behaving any less intrusively. Most tourists are not nasty people or naturally offensive; it simply never occurs to some of us that others may prefer not to have their picture taken. When a lot of money has been spent on a holiday it seems as if we feel we have purchased the right to photograph whatever we want.

I read an account a few years ago of a young mother who drowned while trying to save the life of her six-year-old child in the sea off Mont St Michel. No one offered to help. Tourists with whirring camcorders and snapping cameras looked on and did nothing. One tourist later boasted that he had got the whole thing on tape, and no doubt he found a suitably willing buyer in the media. For me, there was an immediate and obvious parallel with the story of the dying Indian climber on the South Col. Why film his frozen corpse after he had died? What purpose did it serve? And then I thought of photographing the Sadhu lifting rocks up with his penis and wondered if I was just as guilty. Certainly he had grabbed me, encouraged me to part with fifty rupees, exhorted me to take the photographs, but simply by being there with a camera meant that I had created the opportunity for him in the first place. On the other hand, I thought, I wouldn't have missed it for the world. Weight lifting with your happy tackle! No one would believe me if I didn't have a photograph of it.

The noisy hectic bustle of hawkers, rickshaw owners, tourists and traders swamped around me as soon as I stepped outside the temple area. I flagged down an auto-rickshaw, and as it swerved through the congested streets of Kathmandu, I mentally ticked off the tasks that lay ahead of me during the day. I was due to meet Richard Haszko for breakfast at the New Orleans Bar in Thamel. Joining us there would be Liz Hawley, former Reuters correspondent in Nepal, and a walking encyclopaedia on every mountaineering expedition to pass through the country. As joint leaders of a ten-man expedition to climb Pumori by two separate routes, Richard and I had to pass on all the details of our expedition to Liz for her files.

The new Nepalese government rules stipulated that a permit had to be purchased for each specific route as opposed to one for the whole mountain. Richard and five friends wanted to climb Pumori, a 7150-metre peak in the Solo Khumbu, by the popular South-east Face and North-east Ridge, the original line of ascent. Ray Delaney, Ian Tattersall, Ric Potter and I hoped to make an ascent of a new route up what we had named the South Pillar on the right-hand side of Pumori's six-thousand-foot-high South face. Pumori, meaning The Daughter Mountain, was named in honour of George Mallory's daughter Clare. From our base camp the black summit pyramid of Everest looms above the chaos of the Khumbu ice fall with the jagged summits of Lhotse and Nuptse forming a spectacular mountain cirque.

Although tackling different routes, we were all friends

together, and as one group we hoped to save on the cost of
porters, yaks and running base camp. We still had to pay for
two peak permits and expensively equipped Liaison Officers,
as well as more than $7,000 to cover Rescue and Environment
Bonds. It was our job to make sure peak permits, Liaison
Officers, food, fuel and staff were all organised and ready to fly
in to Lukla the day after the rest of the team arrived.

I had been on an expedition to Pumori with Tom in 1991,
and it had ended with the tragic death of Ari Gunnarsson the
day after I left base camp to return home. Attempting to climb
only four months after smashing my left ankle in a 500-foot
fall with Mal Duff on Pachermo, I was not greatly surprised
to find that the unhealed ankle-bone caused me great pain.
Despite using crutches and a special support inside my boot on
the walk-in, the fractured fibula was far too unstable for me
to continue safely and I was forced to abandon the climb.
Instead I sat sunbathing by the base camp lake and, through
binoculars, watched Mal and Liz Duff and Mark Warham
make a successful ascent by the normal route. It was as I
followed their progress up the summit ridge thousands of feet
above me that I first spotted the unclimbed line up the South
Pillar on the right-hand side of the South Face. I was sure no
one had climbed that route before.

'Hey, Joe. Over here.' Richard waved from the corner of
the New Orleans Bar as I picked my way through the scattered
wicker chairs to the sunny spot he had selected.

'Just been watching a bloke lifting up rocks with his knob,'
I said as an opening gambit.

'Charming,' Richard muttered. 'Hasn't put you off your
breakfast then?'

'No, no. Hash browns and Nepali omelette with plenty of
garlic will do me fine. Oh, and a large pot of coffee.'

'Does she know where this place is?' Richard asked,
scanning the bar for Liz Hawley.

'She knows everything,' I said morosely. 'God, I hope she's
got some good news. I'm worried about the route.'

'It'll be fine,' Richard said confidently. 'If anyone knows,
Liz Hawley will.'

'That's what I'm worried about. It's making me feel sick.'

'I think that's probably got more to do with last night's beer.'

Liz Hawley appeared as the first pot of black coffee arrived. She was a long time resident of Kathmandu who had made a point of debriefing virtually every climbing team that passed through. Attempts to avoid her somewhat humourless interrogations usually proved fruitless since she seemed to know where you had been or where you were going before you had opened your mouth or worked it out for yourself. On the other hand, she was also a valuable source of information, and I had heard a disturbing rumour the previous evening about our proposed new route on Pumori. She came directly to the point by flipping a colour photograph on to the break-fast table. On it a felt-tip line marked a route, the writing indicating the various bivouacs and the grade of the ice and rock pitches. I recognised it at once: it was our route, *my* route, the one I had discovered. Every pitch and camp and technical difficulty was exactly as we had envisaged. I lowered my coffee cup with a disbelieving curse.

'That's ours,' I said hoarsely.

'Not any more,' Liz said, in a deadpan voice. 'Czechs, I believe. Leopald Sulovsky and Michalec Zeduak.' She was reading from her notes.

'I don't believe it.' I picked up the photo and stared at it.

'Yes, it was done in the spring. First time.' Liz ignored my despairing look. 'A very strong team as I recall. Two man, Alpine-style and fast.'

'Bastards!' I slumped back, cast my eyes up to the ceiling and felt my hands clench. I wished I hadn't quit smoking.

'You could always repeat it,' Richard said, placing a comforting hand on my shoulder. 'Or switch to our route.'

'To hell with that,' I snapped, pulling away from his touch. 'It's not what we came for. That new line was the only reason for coming back.'

I put my head in my hands and stared hard at the photo-graph on the table, hoping that it might change. 'All that bloody work, three years planning . . .'

'So, what exactly are you lads now going to climb,' Liz Hawley asked in a bright and cheerful manner.

Richard began to explain the complexities of our double team arrangements while I sat there mute and tried to think my way out of the disaster. It wasn't simply that all my hopes and plans were dashed; the rest of the team was due to arrive the following evening and I was going to have to tell them that our route had been done. Would they settle for repeating the route? Possibly, but somehow I doubted it. Ray Delaney had been quite adamant that he didn't want to go anywhere near the normal route. He felt that it was unjustifiably dangerous and the thought of following fixed ropes and countless other teams up the face put him off. Our climbing doctor, Ian Tattersall, I felt sure would prefer to attempt a new route and I couldn't guess what Ric Potter would think about changing lines or making a second ascent. Yet we seemed to have little choice in the matter.

The Nepalese peak permit system did not allow us to change over to any other route that took our fancy. If conditions were impossible or too risky on a chosen line then it was just bad luck and the expedition was over. The inflexibility of the permit system in countries such as Pakistan, India, Tibet and Nepal is the climbers' nightmare. It locks them into a single rigid choice which might tempt them to carry on with an ascent even if their instincts tell them it would be better to switch to another line. If we wished to change our route, it would involve payment of an extra 25 per cent of the $3,000 peak fee. I was damned if I was going to do that, and so in our permit application I had been vague about our route in case we needed to modify or change it.

After Liz had left we finished our breakfast in silence. I pushed my plate away and reached for the coffee pot.

'I'm not sure I can take any more grim predictions and tales of woe.'

'How do you mean?'

'Oh, last night I met Simon Yates and Henry Todd and they were certain that Pumori was going to kill us all,' I replied. 'I can see their point, but it's all a bit much to hear when you haven't even started. Now this news from Liz.'

Simon had been due to lead a group on a guided ascent of Pumori but six months non-stop climbing and travelling had proved too much for him. He was looking pretty strung out with that wild, thousand yard stare of someone who has been on the road for six months too long. Henry Todd, just back from successfully guiding clients up Cho Oyo, the sixth highest mountain in the world, was due to lead a guided ascent of Ama Dablam.

'I thought you had given up on these multiple trips,' I had asked, laughing with delight at seeing him again.

'Well, you know how it is?' Simon muttered sheepishly.

'How come you're going home? I thought you were guiding on Pumori for Henry?'

'So I was, but the trip's cancelled.'

'Why?' I asked, suddenly concerned.

'Too dangerous.' Simon waved a hand nonchalantly and struggled to light his roll-up.

'What?' I spluttered. 'How can you tell?'

'It was cancelled a month ago. Avalanche conditions are lethal at the moment. You know what Pumori is like?'

'Yeah, but you can't tell six weeks in advance.'

'Maybe not, but I'm quite happy,' Simon said with a grin. 'I've just got back from the Khumbu and there's a hell of a lot of snow up there. Ask Henry.'

'Quite right, old boy,' Henry agreed in his charming manner. Still the showman, I thought, as he launched into a long and impassioned explanation of why he thought we would all die under tons of windslab avalanches if we so much as looked at the mountain.

'I hear what you're saying, Henry,' I interrupted him at last, 'and I know Pumori has a dangerous reputation – and that conditions have been bad. Tom and I have just backed off a hill because of them, but we can't very well pull out of this one. The team arrives tomorrow. What do we do? Go fishing instead?'

'Not such a bad idea . . .'

'How come you've cancelled a trip so far in advance? It wouldn't have anything to do with not having enough clients now, would it?' I asked with feigned innocence.

'Not at all. Heaven forbid . . .' Henry replied with a mischievous look in his eye which quickly became one of concern. 'But seriously, mate, just be careful. Okay? I know, and Simon, and a lot of other guys who know these things, say that hill is bloody dangerous at the moment.'

'Okay. I hear you. Thanks Henry.' I raised my beer to him, feeling both grateful and depressed by his advice. 'And the same goes for you on Ama Dablam,' I added, 'those summit slopes can hold a lot of snow.'

'Ah yes,' Henry agreed, 'but everything will be in place by now. You won't believe the number of expeditions on the mountain this season. What is it now – thirteen? And everything's prepared.'

I knew too well what he meant. With so many guided commercial groups as well as private expeditions on the same classic ridge of Ama Dablam, there would be a fixed rope staked, screwed and pegged into place from the ground to the summit. It's the same every season now.

I tried to imagine what the base camp would look like with more than 150 people camped there. When I had climbed the mountain in the spring of 1990, we were the only team there. It meant we could climb it in as good a style as possible. We had elected to fix ropes on the knife-edge horizontal rock ridge between Camps I and II which was a compromise on our original plan to do it entirely Alpine-style. In the event of an accident, trying to retreat back across such ground with an injured friend would be nearly impossible without fixed ropes. The three days' climbing Alpine-style from the top camp had felt serious and committing.

We had been horrified to find the base camp littered with every imaginable item of rubbish. Several pits were filled with tin cans and gas cylinders, while what would burn we gathered together in a great foul pyre, doused with kerosene and incinerated. It took our eight climbers and five Nepali staff several days to clean up the mess. It was interesting to note from the labels on the products that the litter louts came from a broad range of European countries.

With much the same situation probably existing on the normal route on Pumori, I was glad to be trying a new route where no one would have laid a trail out for us. Richard and his team would have to contend with fixed lines at least as far as Camp I. Liz Hawley had said that a Japanese team had already begun their climb ahead of him, and that teams from Korea, the United States, France, Britain, another Japanese team, and possibly teams from Iran and Ireland would soon be heading for Pumori, all intent on climbing the normal route.

Fifteen years ago any expedition to one of these mountains – Everest, Pumori or Ama Dablam – was still a great challenging adventure. Simply getting to Nepal and travelling across it was an achievement, let alone reaching the summit of one's choice. I wasn't sure I liked it now that climbing had become big business.

I wandered distractedly around the streets of Kathmandu, racking my brains for some idea of what to do with our now defunct expedition. In the centre of Thamel I found the barber shop under Tom and Jerry's bar and sank into one of the cracked red leather seats.

'Shave? Massage? Cutting you?' the friendly young barber enquired. I glanced at his smiling reflection in the mirror and saw him eagerly pick up a pair of scissors and look expectantly at the pencil drawings of hair style models pinned on the wall.

'Er, no cutting,' I said hurriedly. 'A shave please.' I remembered the last time he had cut my hair and the battle that ensued when he tried to rid me of grey hairs by liberally dousing my head in what appeared to be boot-black. I had stopped him only in the nick of time.

The man always shaved in the same patterns – down each jaw line, then the cheeks, the bottom lip, firm fingers pinching the cheek up tight as the soft neck is scraped clear of foamy bristles with short jabbing strokes. After that comes the undignified pinch and pull of the nostrils between thumb and forefinger, to stretch the upper lip; and delicate strokes, careful not to catch the corners of the mouth. Then with a reversed blade there comes the barber's version of a backhand stroke, cutting up my lower lip while my eyes are fixed on the mirror, frozen in a paralysed symmetry, staring at the movements of the blade.

Then it was over, and he was wiping the last of the foam

off his blade on to a piece of newspaper. I leant forward to look more closely in the mirror, tentatively touching the deep, diagonal scar that ran through my lip from nostril to mouth, wondering at how he managed never to cut it.

Strong fingers dug through the fabric of the threadbare towel and wiped the last vestiges of foam from the nooks and crannies of my face. As the towel was removed I opened my eyes again in time to see my man administer a resounding blow to the top of my skull, which made me close them again hurriedly. The sound it made was extraordinarily loud and resonant, as if a hollow log had been hit with a dry stick. There was no time to dwell on this interesting thought before he had hit me again in a rapid series of staccato blows that rattled through my skull. The firm crack of his knuckles then abruptly stopped and I felt ten digits digging painfully into my scalp, pressing and scraping and shuddering rapidly back and forth. Then he changed the stroke and pressed one knuckle firmly into the centre of my forehead and began to vibrate it vigorously. I watched myself, almost cross-eyed, as his fist wobbled rapidly from side to side blurring my vision. He caught my eye and smiled broadly.

'Good head massage,' he announced. Then, with a dextrous flip of his hand, he had my head upright and pressed back against his chest as he leaned over the head rest of the chair. In a fluid movement he applied a rapid opposing force to my chin. There was a loud, sickening crack from the base of my neck, and just as swiftly he had reversed hands and was about to repeat the operation in the other direction.

'No cracking,' I managed to yelp before he applied the pressure.

'Ah, yes sir. No problem. No neck breaking,' he said, holding a hand up in apology but with a distinct look of regret that he hadn't been fast enough on the second crack before I protested.

Leaning forward, the barber picked up a large clear crystal from the counter and ran cold water over it before smoothing it across my shaven cheeks. There was a sharp stinging sensation as if he had just rubbed lemon into my face. It felt as if my head had just shrunk. Opening a small tin labelled '*Paris*

Lotion Pomade', he scooped out a liberal dollop of yellowish cream and rubbed it vigorously into my face. The stinging at once receded, to be replaced with an oily feel and a sickly vanilla and lemon fragrance. I saw him dipping his fingers into another container, this one labelled '*Pride and Lovely; The Fairness Cream.*' It was bright pink and smelled like bubble gum and candy floss, with a hint of the scent of rubber erasers in primary school.

I paid him his thirty rupees and left the barber's shop feeling very fair and softened up but no less distracted about the expedition. As I stepped on to the main street I was almost immediately run down by a rickshaw. The passenger looked alarmed, which was understandable since, with only a little newspaper to protect his hands, he was balancing a six-foot by six-foot square pane of glass on his lap. He smiled apologetically at me as I threw myself backwards and the pane narrowly missed my face. An oncoming cyclist veered aside to avoid us and, with a howl of pain, hit his knee against the pedal of a stationary rickshaw.

As I hurried away from the chaotic scene I spotted a large picture in the window of a photographic shop. The familiar buttresses of Pumori's South Face were high-lighted by the setting sun. Ten minutes later I had bought two large photographs and several postcards of the mountain, and was heading for The Blue Note Bar with an unexpected feeling of optimism.

6

Death by Disregard

As part of our acclimatisation on the walk-in to Pumori we spent a rest day at Dingboche, a small settlement nestling under the north face of Ama Dablam. Those of the team who were not suffering from the altitude took the opportunity to explore further up the valley towards the village of Chukung and the site of Island Peak base camp.

I sat in the warm sunshine outside a small lodge in the tiny settlement of Bibre, waiting for Ray to join me and admiring the view. The vast, plunging south face of Lhotse dominated the valley on the left, and to the right the insignificant pyramid of Island Peak was dwarfed by its huge neighbour. At the head of the valley the perfectly symmetrical snow pyramid of Cho Polo glistened in the morning sky.

In front of me the north-west face of Ama Dablam swept up into the sky, draped in hanging glaciers and ice-streaked rock bands. The previous spring it had been climbed by the Czechs, Leopald Sulovsky and Michalec Zeduak. Looking at Ama Dablam now I could see how hard their route was as it zigzagged through sections of vertical ice and over-hanging rock. Five days they had spent forcing their way up the face, and in doing so they had produced the most aesthetic line and technically the hardest ascent that season in the Khumbu.

Their climb was in stark contrast to the hordes of paying clients jumaring their way up the permanently fixed ropes on the south-west ridge. On our walk up to Pangboche from the monastery at Thyangboche the previous day I had watched a long line of black dots inching their way up the fixed ropes on the summit snowfield. Now it seems you only had to clip a jumar on to the ropes fixed by your guides from the summit to the bottom of the route. The cammed teeth of the jumar allowed you to slide it up the rope but locked and gripped the rope tightly when you pulled yourself up. Once the plod to the summit was over you could then slide merrily back down the ropes to camps already set up for you by your Sherpas and eat the hot meals they had prepared. It seemed an odd sort of climbing. It was a shame that this mountain, which is universally regarded as one of the most beautiful in the world, should have become so over-crowded and despoiled, and that people should care so little about how they climbed it.

I glanced back down the valley and saw Ray standing on a small rise adjusting his personal stereo. Behind him the stupendous book-end corner line of Taweche's north face surged dramatically into the morning sky. Basking in the warm sunshine, it was hard to imagine the devastating storm that had swamped this valley only a year earlier.

On 9 November 1995 a freak blizzard hit the Himalaya in Bhutan, Sikkim and Nepal, bringing two days of heavy snowfall which piled up in drifts of between two and three metres deep. Avalanches, floods and landslides caused widespread death and destruction. In Nepal alone the death toll reached 100 by the end of one of the most destructive blizzards in living memory.

By November most expeditions have usually finished climbing, but it is still the height of the trekking season when cold clear weather can be expected and it is rare for such deep snow to fall so low in the mountains. In 1995 the wet and freezing weather caught many trekking groups and their staff unprepared for such wintry conditions. Villages were damaged by avalanches and localised flooding but many trekking parties also took a great deal of punishment. In eastern Nepal, in the region of Kangchenjunga north base camp, three Japanese trekkers and four of their Nepalese staff were killed while their six companions struggled to survive the heavy snowfall. Six Westerners died with many locals when a group of houses were swept away in the Manang region of central Nepal, north of the Annapurna Massif. It is estimated that there were some six thousand trekkers out on the hillsides of Nepal, and a disturbing picture emerged of the neglect by some groups of the safety of their Nepalese staff.

The majority of trekkers visiting the country are relatively inexperienced high mountain travellers who know little or nothing of technical mountaineering and cold weather survival. Some travel in guided groups arranged by trekking agencies, others trek as individuals, perhaps hiring one or two porters to carry and guide for them. Due to keen bargaining for low wages, local porters and agency cook staff are often poorly equipped. Many trekkers seem unaware of their responsibilities and, being inexperienced in the mountains, are unable to help when things go wrong. Some want to save money whatever the cost to others. Many locally employed staff are uninsured for rescue as well as being poorly supplied with good protective warm clothing, footwear and glacier sun-glasses. Instead, bonuses are offered to staff who perform well. These can be substantial, especially for those Sherpas guiding clients on trekking peaks who may receive large bonuses far above their average wages if they reach a summit or a particularly high camp.

A 'Trekking Peak' is a misnomer created by the Nepalese Ministry of Tourism to designate a select group of peaks for which permits are available at a low permit price. Although most of these offer technically easy routes, accessible to a fit winter walker, they remain high mountains of up to 6400 metres, and it is extremely dangerous to underestimate them. With the increasing number of aspiring but inexperienced climbers being brought to the Himalayas by commercial trekking companies, there is a tendency to assume that success is guaranteed because it has been paid for, and the consequent pressure to provide it can result in perilous situations. Bonus payments may lead to parties struggling upwards in worsening weather, despite the prompting of the local guides' better mountaineering instincts. Frostbite injuries can also have a devastating effect on the livelihood of a porter who is utterly dependent on his good health to ensure that he remains on the poverty line and not below it.

At the tiny settlement of Panga, in the Gokyo valley, no more than a long day's walk from our base camp beneath the south face of Pumori, a large group of Japanese trekkers and their staff were sheltering in a cluster of small stone-built summer shelters when a massive avalanche came out of the darkness of the stormy night. The entire Japanese contingent of thirteen trekkers, ten of their eleven Nepalese staff (cooks, guides and porters) as well as two villagers were smothered by the onslaught and killed outright. The single survivor was eventually air-lifted to safety along with the rest of the valley's inhabitants.

It has been said that but for the pressure of the trekking industry this accident would never have occurred. The small shelters used by trekkers would in years past have been evacuated by the locals so late in the season. After the extremes of winter had died away, they would return to these temporary seasonal dwellings, re-roof and rebuild those structures that had been damaged by avalanches and make use of the fresh snow-free pastures. Now that the trekking agencies have dictated that November is high season, the buildings are occupied at a time when for centuries local people have known how vulnerable they are to bad weather. How could one expect poor communities to abandon the advantage of potential profits?

An English climber, Bonny Masson, and her partner John Eames were leading a British trekking group in the Hongu valley, just below the Mera La pass, when the storm broke. Fortunately they had already dismissed their porters, who reached the safety of the high village of Tagnag. The two guides, ten clients and a Sherpa staff of ten were experienced and well equipped and so were able to sit out extremely bad weather for two days at 4900 metres. Masson and Eames had the foresight to camp on a high shoulder which was protected from the constant roar of avalanches on either side. The intimidated Sherpa staff wanted to make a dash through the snowdrifts to join the porters at Tagnag but were persuaded not to do so. Their position was only one day's climb from the high camp on Mera Peak, which they hoped to climb. When the weather improved, after a day and a half of continuous heavy snowfall, the rested and well fed group was able to break out of their sheltered camp and forge a path towards

Tagnag. On the way they came upon parties that had been buried by avalanches on several occasions, others were suffering from severe frostbite injuries in the bitter cold. It took all day to reach Tagnag after dark – a walk that normally takes two hours – wading down icy streams to avoid the treacherous and exhausting snowdrifts on either side.

By the time they arrived there were over a hundred refugees from the storm taking shelter in the small village. When helicopters began to comb the region, some groups requested evacuation, while Masson and Eames led their party on towards the Zatra Og pass, which would eventually bring them down to the safety of Lukla and its airport. Everyone, including their Nepalese staff, had warm clothing and some form of crampons. This was highly unusual. On what would normally be an easy walk they were forced to equip the path with fixed ropes to ensure the group's safety. Despite the enormous avalanche tracks on the path out of Tagnag, the group successfully negotiated the 4595-metre high Zatrwa Og pass where, to her horror, Bonny Masson found the bodies of four porters who had fallen victims to hypothermia or falls and had been abandoned by their trekking groups. One had been sent back to retrieve a dropped trek bag. Another young Rai porter, wearing the ubiquitous ankle-length rubber boots and thin cotton trousers, was found frozen to death with his load of Westerner's equipment still on his back; some of that equipment – down clothing and Gore-Tex jackets – might have saved his life. Bonny Masson gently covered the porter's body so as not to upset members of her own group.

Further east on that stormy night the British explorer and trek leader, Steve Razzetti, reported seeing a Japanese party camped beside his group at Pang Pema beneath the North Face of Kangchenjunga. A misty halo around the moon and thin bands of high cirrus convinced him that a serious blizzard would soon be upon them and that it was time to start making their way down. While Steve began the descent next morning, the Japanese leader ignored his warnings and chose to stay at Pang Pema in the hope of a clearing and the fabulous view of Kangchenjunga. Since they were well equipped and provisioned, Steve thought no more about it.

High cirrus clouds, rushing across the sky, were replaced by an unbroken layer of high cloud with ominous lenticular cloud caps curling over the surrounding summits. As the weather steadily deteriorated during the day Steve passed several large groups still heading up the valley. Many of the ascending porters were silent and dispirited, most were wearing shorts or cotton trousers, flip-flops and large rectangles of polythene as a waterproof to keep their loads dry.

Thirty-six hours and several metres of snow later, Steve's group found itself waking to a perfect sunny day in the village of Khambachen. The villagers were setting about the grim tasks of saving first their houses and then their livestock. Over a hundred yaks, the lifeblood of the village, had perished in the storm. While Steve and his group spent the day fighting their way down to the next settlement of Ghunsa, making sure that they all stayed together, the Japanese at Pang Pema were coming to terms with the loss of seven Nepalese staff and three trekkers in an avalanche. That afternoon the constant bustle of helicopters in the mountain skies signalled that the biggest rescue operation in Nepalese history was under way. Steve Razzetti, like Bonny Masson and John Eames, managed to lead his clients and staff to safety because of his experience and foresight. He did not distinguish, as other groups did, between clients and Sherpas. In his eyes they were all the same.

For many days afterwards, long lines of Sherpas arrived at the Khunde hospital in the Khumbu with terrible injuries and stories of how they had been abandoned by their clients. Some men lost their entire limbs to frostbite. In the Annapurna region, between Damphus and Frenchman's Pass on the Dhaulagiri circuit, a trekking party abandoned six of their snowblind porters in the storm. They all died.

Whatever happened to the age-old sense of concord thought common to mountaineers and sailors in the face of death and distress? I had always thought that natural disasters tended to break down cultural barriers and fostered a spirit of unity between people of all nations and races as they worked together to survive. It doesn't seem to exist today – at least, not in the modern world of mountaineering. These clients of trekking companies are not mountaineers; they have served no apprenticeship in the hills, have learned nothing of the ethos of behaviour that governs any true mountain lover. Many of them show no respect for the mountains, nor for the people who struggle to live among them. For some the mountain arena has become no more than a glorified theme park from which they can buy their exit whenever they wish, and for whatever reason, whether boredom or fear.

In one way, it was a natural disaster, a risk that all mountain dwellers face. The loss of agricultural land and livestock can eventually be replaced, even though a yak represents the equivalent of a Nepalese teacher's annual salary. Buildings can be repaired or relocated. People and their trust in others are less tangible losses, and the hardest to replace. The traditionally generous disposition of the Nepalese mountain peoples towards visiting climbers and trekkers may well have been irrevocably damaged by what took place in the November storm of 1995. People from rich western nations showed what they really cared about – themselves. Some trekkers, faced with the cost of £200 per head to evacuate by helicopter, chose to leave behind their Nepalese staff to fend for themselves as they boarded the aircraft. They didn't even have the decency to leave their expensive protective clothing for those people who, only days before, had been waiting on them hand and foot. The staff, it would appear, were simply a commodity that could be bought and thrown away without a second thought.

*

Leaning back against the sun-warmed stone walls, I glanced up the valley towards the settlement of Chukung. Then Ray appeared, smiling broadly.

'Remember this,' he said with a grin and a majestic sweep of the hand.

'No,' I said.

'What do you mean, no? We were here in . . .'

'Yes, I know that, but if you recall we couldn't see a hand in front of our faces for most of the time. In fact, the only good view we had was from the summit of Island Peak. And that lasted all of five minutes.'

'Yeah, I think we were the only ones who saw it,' Ray said. 'Do you remember that guy Brendan and Kate were hauling up? By the time they had got him to the top, all they could see was cloud.'

'The squaddie.' I chuckled. 'He couldn't even remember getting to the top . . .'

'After all that load-carrying as well,' Ray agreed. 'What did he think he was proving by carrying those huge loads all the way in from Jiri while we took only our day sacks?'

'All macho and no brains,' I said as Richard joined us at the lodge. 'Hi there. How's tricks?'

'Not bad.' He swung his rucksack from his shoulders as Bruce French ambled up the path behind him.

'You don't seem to be bothered by the altitude,' I said as he flopped down beside me.

'No, I feel great.'

'Bloody typical!' Richard muttered, wiping the sweat from his brow. 'Spends his whole life playing cricket and then wanders up here as if it's just a stroll round the park.' Bruce laughed at Richard's pretence of jealousy.

'What do you think, eh?' Ray said, nodding at the sweep of Lhotse's south face.

'Unbelievable.' Bruce gazed in awe at the fourth highest mountain in the world.

'We're going to head on up to Chukung. Are you two coming?' Richard asked us as he finished off his glass of lemon tea.

'I'm quite happy here,' Ray said. 'What do you think, Joe?'

'This will do me,' I replied. 'See you two at Dingboche later. Don't overdo it now.'

Ray and I watched as they dwindled to small specks, lost against the green and brown dry hillside. Chukung was less than an hour's walk from where we rested. During the previous autumn, the whole valley had been choked with snow, and Chukung had been almost buried. The snow piled up level with the roofs, but those fortunate enough to be caught there by the storm were safe in the warmth and security of the solid stone houses. Further up the valley, at the site of Island Peak base camp, people were fighting for their lives as avalanches thundered down from the surrounding slopes.

Disparate groups formed into a column of trekkers and Sherpa staff trying to force their way out of the deadly trap that the base camp had become. It was to take days rather than hours for the groups to break out. In the dark an avalanche rushed down on them burying three of the Sherpas who were at the back of the retreating column. Digging frantically in the maelstrom, they managed to find two of the victims and revive them. The survivors were then forced to abandon the search for the third victim and continue their desperate retreat. The buried Sherpa was fortunate enough to be able to dig himself out and eventually managed to catch up with the slow-moving column.

Later, as the bedraggled and exhausted party struggled down a partly frozen stream, which offered faster progress than ploughing through the drifts, a young cook-boy fell into the freezing water and was completely submerged. Despite frantic efforts to get him out of his frozen clothes and into the warmth of a sleeping bag he died before his trousers were off. The party spent the next day and night fighting their way down the valley, and yet, when found, they were still only a kilometre from where the boy had died.

Two Swedish women were the first to reach Chukung and sound the alarm. Camped in a relatively sheltered spot, they had heard screams and cries of despair after the roar of the avalanches had receded. They quickly discovered that conditions were too severe for them to effect a rescue attempt on their own. They nearly died in their struggle to get to Chukung, where a group of Sherpas and Western climbers were already trying to break trail towards those stranded at the base camp. Wading through chest-high drifts and taking it in turns to open the trail, the rescue party was in constant danger of being caught in avalanches sweeping down from what two days before had been dry hillsides. On the second day they came upon the exhausted Swedish survivors who had made a dash from their base camp.

After the Swedes had been escorted down to the village, two more of their companions were found, as well as two snowblind Sherpas wearing their socks as gloves. Another Sherpa was discovered slumped in the snow, blind, with frozen hands, and bare feet. A pair of boots was found in his load.

The weary band of rescuers then came across two Americans and their Sherpa guide sitting in the snow. They had rushed to leave the camp three days earlier when the snow first began to fall heavily. In the rush they had left vital equipment behind in the hope that they could reach Chukung by travelling light. They hadn't anticipated the severity of the storm or the exhausting work of trying to break trail through such terrain at four and a half thousand metres.

Eventually the injured and exhausted groups of Swedes and Americans were evacuated by helicopter. All the injured locals were flown out under the American insurance. A group of Germans trapped at the Island Peak base camp were eventually taken out to safety by helicopter.

One distressing incident in this storm illustrates the selfishness of some of the trekkers. Two Western clients had abandoned their Sherpa when he was too weak to move from his tent to the helicopter. The clients broke trail out to the aircraft, which had been unable to land nearby, and then took off, leaving the poor man to die. When asked in Namche why they had abandoned the Sherpa, the same trekkers had replied that they were anxious to reach the airport at Lukla so that they would not miss their international flight connections. These people had bought themselves into a dream trip, and when that dream became a nightmare, they simply bought themselves out, displaying a total lack of responsibility and humanity. Money talks.

7

To the Moon and Back

The line of chortens stood like sentinels silhouetted against a stark horizon of ice peaks, sombre stone plinths surrounded by some of the world's most beautiful mountains. Ama Dablam, Tamserku, Kantaiga, Taweche and Cholatse formed a stupendous wall of ice and rock, piercing the freezing azure sky behind them. On each chorten was a name, sometimes many names, and dates, and occasionally a few poignant words of tribute to the departed. At the head of the valley the cause of all this loss reached highest into the frosty sky. The dark summit pyramid of Everest, reaching far above the encircling Nuptse-Lhotse walls, caught the mid-morning sun. That morning it was a black wedge against the sky, with sunshine glittering through huge plumes of ice crystals that were blowing north into Tibet, rolling in great boiling swirls up and over the summit snows like silent surf bursting over an unseen reef. High overhead thin streaks of cloud, tell-tale signs of an impending storm front, raced to fill the sky. At the head of the Khumbu banks of dark cloud had filled the glacier valley and were surging in a heavy swell up towards the summit of Nuptse. Within half an hour a dark sinister lenticular cloud would suction itself to the summit ridge and hold position, darkening with every minute. Eventually the sun would vanish behind a rising wall of storm clouds. As the air became frosty and the first snow flakes danced around me on the wind I walked towards the nearest chorten, curious to read the name on it.

'Hannelore Schmatz, 1979.' There were some other words, inscribed faintly in German, which I could not read. The remnants of a sun-bleached prayer flag fluttered in the wind and traces of dark ashes, probably burnt juniper, filled the small hole set into the chimney-like structure of the chorten. It was a shock to recognise the name. I didn't know her but had heard about her death. She was the fifth woman to climb Everest and she had died with her partner, the American climber Ray Genet, while descending from the summit. Exhausted by the climb, they had stopped to bivouac high above the South Col as night approached, despite the exhortations of their Sherpa companions. Genet had disappeared in the snows but, by some freak accident, Hannelore's body was swept further down from their last bivouac and for several years it had remained a grisly landmark on the South-east Ridge. On his weary descent from an impressive climb at the age of fifty in 1985, Chris Bonington described spotting what he thought was a tent as he approached the South Col and veered towards the dark shape. To his horror, he realised as he drew near that it was the figure of a woman, sun-bleached hair blowing in the wind, staring sightlessly across the frozen horizon of peaks. She was eventually swept away and buried, free from the gaze of the hundreds of people that were soon to follow her tracks to the summit. No longer was she to be a grim addition to a passing climber's slide collection.

I looked up at the line of chortens, stepping away across the hillside, like silent smokeless chimneys, and thought of all the names inscribed there, all the lost hopes. It was a moving sight, and I was glad to find that I was on my own, ahead of the rest of the team. I sat and absorbed the view, thinking of all the sad and lonely places where I had found memorials and grave sites in the mountains. I remembered the lone grave on Antisana, planted with wild mountain flowers, with condors swinging on thermals above the volcanoes on the horizon, and scattered white headstones on the massive icy flanks of Chimborazo. In the Cordillera Blanca of the Peruvian Andes I had found two dilapidated crosses amidst the rusting tin cans and discarded rubbish of Pisco's high camp and made a small and seemingly futile effort to clear up the mess.

Only last Christmas, while staggering up loose scree slopes in the pitch black of a summer night on Mt. Kenya, I had suddenly come upon a great mound of stones loosely piled up. At first, in the stygian gloom, I did not recognise it for what it was and sat upon it as a welcome chance to rest. My companion, a Dutch friend and mountain guide called Rob Steenmeijer, was a distant flickering yellow head-torch. As I rose to follow him I spotted the small cross and realised I had been sitting on someone's grave. I knelt on the mound of rocks and peered at a small glass frame covering a sheet of red paper. It gave a name that I can no longer remember, and an age, twenty-five, and a date, 1960. It struck me more poignantly because, by coincidence, the year of this young climber's death was the year of my birth, and he had died at the same age that by rights I should have died on Siula Grande in Peru. I wondered what misfortune had killed him – altitude sickness, rock fall, avalanche? I wondered, too, whether he had been approaching the same climb as we were, the Diamond Couloir on Mt. Kenya, a serious ice climb, especially in the thin conditions of an African summer. I found it hard to avoid thinking of that lonely grave on our ascent over the next two days.

The panorama of mountains that formed a backdrop to the line of chortens was dominated by the immaculate symmetry of Ama Dablam gleaming in the morning sun. The mountains seemed tranquil and pristine. I found it hard to connect them with these grim memorials to climbers who had died. In that distant bright horizon all I could see was beauty and adventure and fun. As I stood up and turned, hefting my rucksack across my shoulders, storm clouds could be seen streaming from the summit of Pumori across to Everest and Nuptse, icy fingers clawing across the sky, bringing with them freezing blizzard winds and heavy snow. I put my head down and hurried on towards the yak pastures at Gorak Shep and the final moraines above our Pumori base camp, anxious to get the tents up before the weather closed in completely.

By mid-day the tents were pitched on individual platforms excavated from the rough moraines bordering the double lake that marked the base camp. At its furthest tip there was a sandy beach a few hundred yards from where we were camped. I remembered it as the place where we had camped five years before. Our yaks had arrived, the stores were unloaded and some of the yaks were driven over to the beach area.

'There's a lot of snow,' Tom said shading his eyes as he looked up. 'See those crown walls?'

'Look up there, to the left of the col,' Ric said, pointing to the thin shadow lines showing where avalanches had broken away. 'Just below the cloud level.' Ray came over and handed his binoculars to Tom who scanned the slopes, trying to work out whether the whole face had avalanched and was therefore now safe.

'I don't like it,' I said flatly. 'Henry Todd said he'd seen some enormous avalanches when he was on Everest. The whole thing pluming off in all directions after a storm, as if she had shaken her shoulders and dumped the lot.' I squinted at the glare of the south face and shook my head. 'There's a hell of a lot of snow.'

'Yeah, too much,' Tat agreed. 'Even that central rock buttress is plastered and the summit slopes above it look frightening.'

'What's going on over there?' I asked Tom, nodding towards the beach. 'Who are those guys?'

'Koreans, I think,' Tom replied. 'Although they could be Japanese. They're using our yaks for the walk out.'

'I heard a trekker in Gorak Shep mention that the normal route has just been climbed,' Ric shouted from where he was struggling to erect his tent.

'Yes, I think you're right. I heard that some of the Japanese team topped out.'

'More like their Sherpas,' Richard interrupted sharply.

'Yeah, that's true.' Tom nodded towards the beach. 'There's no sign of the Americans on Bill Crouse's team. I think they must be camped higher up, over that ridge.' He pointed to the east where the start of the normal route lay.

'So, it has been climbed anyway?' I asked. 'Despite all the dire warnings about deadly avalanches.'

By the evening it was snowing hard and would continue to do so for the next five days. I began to fear that, just as in the Langtang on Gangchempo in 1993, we were going to be snowed out before even setting foot on the mountain. We made a few forays up towards the base of the south face, carrying heavy loads of personal gear, ropes, hardware, stoves, propane gas, and tents and stashing them beneath some prominent boulders near the edge of the glacier. We were pleased to discover it took a little over an hour to reach the site of the cache, from which Ray and I made an exploratory sortie up on to the glacier. It appeared to be safe and virtually free of crevasses.

After the second day of driving snow the jagged moraines upon which we had camped were carpeted in a smooth white cloak of powder which hid the ankle-breaking rocks beneath. As I trudged up the short slippery incline towards the mess tent, I noticed that the line of prayer flags from the *puja* ceremony was collapsing under the weight of snow. The altar had completely disappeared.

'Hell fire,' I said, knocking the snow from my shoulders as I ducked through the doorway. 'This had better stop soon.' I glanced at the long table laden with steaming tea pots, pans of porridge and plates of freshly baked Tibetan breads around which everyone sat.

'Well, at least we're safe here,' Ray said. 'No chance of being avalanched.'

'Just slowly buried,' Tat muttered morosely.

'I spent all night thinking about it,' Richard said. 'There were twenty-five people killed near here in a single avalanche last year.'

'You mean in the Gokyo Valley?' I said.

'Remember the huge dump of snow that took out all those people at Island Peak base camp?' Richard added. 'That was in the autumn as well. October 19 1987, I think it was.'

'Yeah, but that mainly involved climbers. It was nothing like last year, and people didn't behave so badly either.'

A week later, we were still sitting in base camp, wondering whether yet another big storm was about to sweep in. Fortunately the persistent snowfall and constant cloud cover were not so bad as to keep us pinned down in the tents. We made several forays up towards a prominent boulder close to the start of the glacier where we could make a dump of equipment. Richard Haszko's team – Bruce French, Tony Halliwell, Tom Richardson and Karen Grunberg – set about establishing their advanced base camp for the normal route beside the American tents at 5800 metres.

Apart from the weather, sickness had also struck the camp. The sixth member of the normal route team, Steve Hartland, a guide from Plas-y-Brenin, the National Outdoor Centre in North Wales, was recuperating further down the valley, having been diagnosed as suffering from a pulmonary oedema. Tat was coughing badly from a chest infection, and Ric was feeling weak from the altitude. Ric had suffered a pulmonary on Mt. Kenya several years before and was understandably anxious about his condition. For once, I felt fit and strong, and raring to go, but instead was forced to sit out the bad weather, worrying about the mountain.

To add to our woes, we seemed to be losing kitchen staff at an incredible rate. Our Sirdar had left us on the first day, after we had paid our agent nearly a thousand dollars for his services. It meant that in the event of a serious accident requiring helicopter rescue we had no one left with the authority to radio Kathmandu for rescue.

Our Liaison Officers should have been there to do this for us but they hadn't bothered to turn up at base camp, despite our paying them nearly $2,500 in wages. Amrit, our cook, was coughing almost as badly as Tat. One of the cook boys had been sent back to Namche to try to find the cooking oil and cheese that had mysteriously disappeared from the yaks on the walk-in. Nima had been sent to purchase potatoes and hadn't been seen for days. Pasang was keeping Steve company in Deboche, and Pertemba had a bad chest infection and was told by Tat to descend the next day.

Ray, Ric and I waited as Tat made slow progress up the loose and tiring scree near the dump. He had been coughing heavily and paused frequently to rest. I suspected that he had picked up the same chest infection as Amrit, our cook. Antibiotics were almost useless at the height of our base camp, where the body struggles to fight even relatively minor infections. I was worried about Tat.

124

'Are you all right?' I asked him as we piled the gear into a voluminous haul bag and weighted it down with rocks.

'Yeah, but struggling a bit with my chest,' he wheezed. 'Should be over it soon.'

'Why not go down for a bit?' Ric suggested.

'I thought about it, but it doesn't seem too bad,' Tat said.

I laughed. 'Until you try and walk uphill that is. Fat lot of good that's going to do you.'

'It's just that I don't want to get out of sync with the rest of you.'

'Well, I'm not feeling too good either,' Ric said. 'Sleeping badly and feeling breathless, so you've not much to stay in sync with.'

'And it's snowing like buggery.' I pointed to the grey ice-sheathed screes and boulders. 'None of us will be climbing anything in a hurry. Why not let Ray and I make a few more carries up here while you recuperate. You don't have to go all the way to Namche. You could get to Pheriche in half a day and lose over a thousand metres. That should be enough.'

'Yeah, well, I'll see how it goes,' Tat muttered without committing himself.

'You should know,' I said, 'you are the doctor. But re-member what happened to me on Cho Oyo,' I warned as we headed down into a wet snow-laden wind. After a short while Tat stopped for a good purgative whooping hack.

'Physician! Heal thyself,' I yelled at the crouched figure and chuckled as he raised his finger.

Meanwhile, Richard and his team had carried loads up to the site of their advanced base camp and set up a couple of two-man tents on a sheltered platform. It was a two-and-a-half hour walk away to the east and over a thousand feet above the base of our route on the face. They had met the American team and learned some surprising facts about the recently departed Japanese. It appeared that the latter's Sherpa team had fixed and staked ropes all the way to the prominent col on the north-east ridge, as well as establishing and stocking advanced base camp and then Camp I at 6200 metres. During this entire period the Japanese themselves had not set foot on the mountain. Only after their exasperated

Sirdar had eventually come down to explain to them that the only way they could possibly climb the mountain was to leave the security of their mess tent did they actually start up the ropes. Of the four who set off, one became ill – unaccustomed as they were to the altitude – while the other three, it seemed, were virtually dragged up by their climbing Sherpa staff.

'What sort of climbing is that?' I asked incredulously.

'It isn't,' Ray said bluntly.

'It's pretty unfair on the Sherpas,' Richard added. 'They do all the work and then have to risk their necks dragging the buggers up.'

'Ah, yes, but the pay is good,' I said sarcastically.

'That's got nothing to do with it,' Ray snapped. 'It's still not climbing, is it? It's as if they had bought the bloody mountain.'

'Well, they had, to all intent and purpose, and so have we.'

'Come off it,' Ric said. 'We've just paid for a peak permit. We aren't using Sherpa guides or high altitude porters. We're doing all our own climbing. It's hardly the same. Besides, fixed ropes are an integral part of Himalayan climbing, and always have been.'

'Maybe, but you didn't use them on your new route on Kwangde, did you?' I retorted. 'And, if you do use them, you should at least climb up and fix them yourself. It seems pretty retrograde to me to go climbing peaks like Pumori with more ropes and logistic support than was used thirty or more years ago on the first ascents,' I said plaintively.

'It makes you wonder what they're doing it for, what their motives are,' Ray said. 'I mean, they must be different from ours?'

'Why?' Tat demanded. 'They want to climb the mountain, just as we do. They simply have a different perspective on what is an acceptable way of doing it. It doesn't mean they are wrong and we are right.'

'Well, maybe,' I agreed reluctantly, 'but the truth is that if guiding wasn't allowed, then people who are not climbers, who haven't got enough skills, wouldn't be able to climb these hills in any old style now, would they?'

'Yes, but what's wrong with guiding?' Tom said as he sat down at the mess tent table with a steaming cup of coffee. 'Why shouldn't everyone have the chance to climb these mountains?'

'You have a trekking company, so you would say that,' I retorted, and immediately regretted it.

'Yes, and you've guided with me in Peru,' Ric countered. 'So what's the difference?'

'Okay, but we took people up things they *could* climb without fixed ropes. We didn't make the mountain easier or smaller for them, and maybe they learned something doing it.'

'In a way, they are lying to themselves,' Richard put in. 'It's like cheating at a game. If no one sees you, well, you might get away with it, but inside you will always know you've cheated, and you'll never forget it.'

'And what's that got to do with guiding?' I asked.

'Take what happens on Everest,' Ray continued. 'I'll bet, with the light-weight Russian bottles they have today, some clients use more oxygen on an ascent from the South Col than Hillary and Tenzing ever did.'

'Yeah,' I said, laughing. 'Someone once called it climbing Everest with enough oxygen to get to the moon and back!'

Ray laughed too. 'Don't get me wrong. I'm not saying it's easy, far from it.'

'Oh sure, I know everyone calls it the *Yak Trail* but I'll bet it's bloody hard work. It might be a great achievement for the individual but as far as mountaineering significance is concerned, it's not.'

'And it's still *not* climbing,' Ray said forcefully. 'Letting someone else do all the work, fix the ropes, carry the loads and then guide you up the thing is not climbing.'

'Was it Doug Scott who said . . . *if you're not making your own decisions, you are not a climber*?' I added.

'Quite,' Ray agreed. 'It's back to Richard's cheating argument. You didn't do the requisite things to get you to the top, someone else did. And on an even more basic level you used oxygen, which effectively reduces the true height of the mountain by a thousand metres or more, depending on the flow rate. So in the end you haven't climbed a 29,028-foot hill but one about 26,028-foot high. Quite a difference, I'd say.'

'Isn't it a bit unfair to insist that everyone has to climb in the best possible style just because Messner and Habeler did?' Tom threw in the question.

'Why?' I was determined not to be put off. 'We insist on it in rock climbing. Even sport-climbing seems to have a better ethical approach. What's wrong with being led by the elite, aspiring to be the very best? What's wrong with elitism, for God's sake?'

'It's totalitarian.'

'Eh? How?'

'Because it takes away people's choices to do things that they want to do. If they want to use fixed ropes, it is their free choice. Elitism dictates to people.'

'Hang on,' Ray said. 'People draping fixed ropes on a route takes away other climbers' choice to climb it Alpine-style.'

'It's no different to having rules for any other game,' I pointed out. 'I mean, if you want to win an Olympic gold medal or a Wimbledon singles final, you have to do two things: play by the rules and play well enough to win. You can't change the rules just to suit your lesser abilities. What would be the point?'

'Who was it that said you must always strive to make an ascent in the same style, or *better*, than the last ascensionist?' Ray asked.

'Royal Robbins, or was it Harding?' I suggested.

'It was Royal Robbins, and his principles of ascent,' Richard replied.

'Anyway,' I snapped. 'What does it matter who said it. It's the sense of it that counts.'

'I thought climbing was supposed to be free from rules and regulations,' Tat said. 'The whole attraction is its anarchy.'

'Yes, but as Joe said earlier, these clients we're talking about are not climbers, are they? Not by Doug Scott's definition anyway,' Richard added smugly. 'So they either don't care or simply don't know that they should be striving to do it in any better style. If jumaring gets them up a hill, then to them that's climbing. QED.'

'Well, it shouldn't be allowed,' I muttered.

'There's room for all of us, surely,' Ric said in such a reasonable tone of voice. 'I mean, real climbers will always know the score, so what does it matter if others are not perfect. They climb their way, we climb ours. Anyway, we aren't exactly saints.'

'If you think that, then you might as well say anything goes in athletics,' I almost shouted. 'Forget the rules, he's the fastest on drugs and he's the fastest not on drugs, so we'll give a medal to both of them . . .'

'Not a bad idea!' Richard said.

'Yeah, and we could also allow third division footballers to handle the ball out of choice, just because they aren't as good as the premier league players . . .'

'Come off it, Joe,' Ric snapped.

'Okay, so it's not a good analogy. What I mean is that by having a right and a wrong way of doing things, we have a standard by which to measure our performance, and people can't easily ruin the whole sport and put other people's lives in jeopardy through negligence. It's no more than the basic ethic of doing as you would be done by.'

'And without these standards it would be chaos,' Ray added. 'Just think of what would happen to rock climbing at home if we had no standards . . .'

'Exactly,' I agreed. 'Just imagine what would happen to all the traditional routes, like *Indian Face* if that happened. A typical Johnny Dawes route – very thin, minimal protection, totally committing, with maximum death potential – if you screw up, you're stuffed. None of us would dare try it, unless of course we bolted it and made it safe. Then we could all climb it after practising the moves. But what would that prove?'

'Bugger all,' Ray muttered.

'We would have destroyed a piece of Johnny's brilliance, his genius for climbing. I mean, hell, it wasn't repeated for nearly ten years. We won't climb *Indian Face* because we aren't good enough, or brave enough, or visionary enough. If we bolted it and brought it down to our level, we'd destroy the whole point of it, strip it of the very reason why it was such a brilliant achievement. And that is what's happening here.'

'I don't know why this is bugging you all of a sudden,' Ric said. 'You've never mentioned it before, so what's changed?'

'Maybe I didn't bother to think about it before,' I replied guardedly. 'And maybe I hadn't realised quite how low people are prepared to stoop to climb things like that,' I added, nodding towards Everest.

'So why now?'

'I don't know,' I muttered. 'Everest, I suppose. The way the Dutch left that man to die, and the Indians being left to die last spring, and the November storms with so many Sherpas abandoned. It sickens me really. I keep thinking it's the thin edge of a wedge that will just ruin everything.'

'A couple of instances of bad behaviour is no reason to condemn the whole thing,' Tom said reasonably.

'Oh I know that, and I suppose it was inevitable with the numbers of people now coming here.'

'So what are you doing here?' Tat asked succinctly.

'Good question . . . no, unfair one, actually. We planned this trip years ago, long before I thought this way.' I paused. 'It just seems that something has changed, something is wrong here now. I don't like it any more.'

'Well, what a brilliant time to come to that conclusion,' Richard said with a laugh, peering out at the snow swirling on the wind past the flapping mess tent door. I laughed as well.

'After all this breast-beating the acid test, of course,' Tat said, 'is this: if someone offered you a free trip to Everest with the most expensive and therefore successful commercial expedition, would you take it? It would involve fixed ropes and oxygen and everything, and therefore – for a climber of your ability – offer a very good chance of reaching the summit. Would you take it?'

'No,' I said firmly. 'No, well, I hope I wouldn't . . . I mean . . . I'm not . . .'

'Sure.' Tat completed the sentence with a laugh.

'It's completely hypothetical. I mean it just wouldn't happen . . .'

'Yes, but you still can't say for certain that you would refuse to go.'

'I can say what I would like my decision to be. Or I could accept and try to climb it without oxygen and . . .'

'And if you found you couldn't, would you then use it?'

'I don't know. I hope I'd have the integrity not to, but I can't say for sure, can I? At least I might have tried to do it in a good style . . .'

'That's a bit soft.'

'It's also unfair,' I retorted. 'Do I want to climb Everest? Have I ever wanted to? As a kid, yes, as an adult, not much, no. Would I want to organise a trip, raise the money, slog up the ropes, take the risks to be the six hundred and whatever person up there? No . . . but if someone offered it to me on a plate, gratis, well, I . . . to be honest, I don't know.' I finished lamely to general laughter. 'It's not as simple as that,' I protested to even louder cries of derision.

'Tea ready,' Pertemba announced as he pushed through the door flaps with two large thermos flasks of tea. I stood up and went out for a pee, hunching my shoulders against the driving snow as I ducked out of the door.

Tat, Ray, Ric and I had spent the best part of four days arguing about the new route and the style in which we wanted to climb it. After learning from Liz Hawley that our new line had already been climbed, I had made a mad dash around the Kathmandu bookshops, poring over as many books of glossy colour photos as I could find in the hope of spotting another feasible line on the face that we could still legitimately climb under the vague description I had given for the peak permit. I spotted a great buttress running up the centre of the face which, as far as I could ascertain, was still unclimbed. Unfortunately the crux of the climbing was up one thousand feet of vertical rock, and we were geared to climb an ice and mixed route. I had faxed home in time for the others to bring out some extra equipment, but with the heavy snow, even this route looked an unlikely prospect.

'I still say it's our safest option,' I argued. 'For a start, we can climb on the rock buttress, which no one else can do, while waiting for the snow conditions to improve.'

'Yeah, but what's the point of that?' Tat asked. 'Even if we climb the buttress and then get up the crest of the ridge above, we are all agreed that the summit slopes look lethal. So why start up something we know we can't finish?'

'We could always swop to the normal route if we had to,' Ric suggested. 'After all, our Liaison Officers won't know, will they? I'll bet they're still in Namche.'

'At the Bada Dasain festival in Kathmandu, more likely,' Ray said. 'Anyway, count me out of the normal route. I don't want anything to do with it.'

'Nor me,' I agreed, thinking of Ari. 'It's an option for some of us if we fail on the face but we have to give the route a try first.'

'Listen,' Tat said, nodding at Ric. 'Last time the weather was clear we saw a possible line to the right of the Czech route, all snow, a bit of mixed. It wasn't bad. It looked the easiest line, relatively safe, depending on the snow, of course.'

'You know, that crescent-shaped buttress sweeping up to the right of those rocks above the pear-shaped buttress,' Ric added. He pointed out the line on the photographs and post-cards of the face that I had brought with me.

'This whole bloody expedition has gone pear-shaped,' I muttered. 'And it's not as good as the Czech route . . .'

'Yes, I hadn't appreciated how good that was from the photos,' Ray said. 'It's a classic line, isn't it? And the steep ice sections look magnificent.'

'I know, I know, don't go on about it,' I snapped. 'I feel bad enough to know we lost it without you telling me how wonderful it is.'

'We could load carry right up to the base of the pear buttress even in this weather and make up our minds when it improves.' Tat, as always, provided the most reasonable and logical option.

'Well, I suppose if we don't do that, we might as well go home now,' I agreed morosely.

'Cheer up,' Ric said, laughing at me. 'It could be worse.'

'You're kidding! How could it be worse, for God's sake?'

After another night of heavy snow, Ric decided to go down with Pertemba. We were left with a sick cook and no other staff, and Tat was looking decidedly rough. Steve Hartland turned up with Pasang, having recovered from his pulmonary oedema, but Pasang went straight down again with similar symptoms. I'd never seen such a sickly looking bunch. The next morning Tat appeared at breakfast with a puffed up face that looked as if it had been attacked by a thousand hornets. Only the distinctive nose was recognisably Tat, and there were strange rashes all over his chest and arms.

'Got to go down,' he said, lighting a cigarette and coughing furiously. 'I feel dreadful.'

'You look dreadful,' Richard exclaimed sympathetically. 'Keep away from me.'

'You've got a head like a pumpkin,' someone added.

'I always thought you were ugly but this takes the biscuit . . .'

'Bugger off, the lot of you,' Tat responded to our friendly banter. My heart went out to him. He knew that the trip was over for him before he had climbed a foot of the route. I knew how he felt.

'I think you're going to be a bit out of sync now, mate,' I said quietly as Tat packed his gear outside his tent. 'By the time you get back it will be too late. It's tough, but Ray and I can't afford to wait . . .' I trailed off, with an embarrassed grimace.

'I know, don't worry,' Tat said, peering at me through puffy eyes. 'What's so bloody funny?'

'Oh, I don't know. You look awful.' I shook my head. 'If I didn't laugh, I'd cry. I mean, look at us. In less than a week we have lost our new route, most of our Nepali staff and half our team. There's just Ray and me left, and we haven't even decided which route we're going to do or in what style.'

'Yes, it is pretty daft,' Tat agreed.

'I told you to go down. You should have listened,' I insisted. 'You're even more stubborn than I am. And you're the flipping doctor . . .'

'Yeah, okay, don't rub it in,' Tat said wearily. 'It's not the chest any more. Something else has happened. I think it's an allergic reaction to the anti-biotics I was taking.'

'Sorry, look I didn't mean it like that . . .' I trailed off. I was angry not with Tat but with the circumstances. I really enjoyed climbing with him, and we would miss his quiet good humoured manner.

Ray and I said our farewells before heading up to the foot of the face, intent on carrying loads to the base of the pear-shaped buttress and maybe reconnoitring a route up the crescent-shaped snow slope on its right-hand side. We had elected in the end to attempt the route Tat and Ric had seen but we felt vulnerable now that we were at half strength. Reports from Richard's team and the Americans suggested that avalanche conditions were not quite as bad as everyone had feared. We had to hope that the same was true for the area of the face that we were attempting.

8

Little White Lies

At last it looked as if the weather had broken. High cirrus clouds, the reaching talons of yet another frontal system, had been racing across the sky all day in jet stream winds far above the summit of Pumori, which itself looked fearsome in its fresh cloak of snow. Heavier clouds massed ominously in the south west, but by evening they had receded, and I could see from my altimeter that the pressure was remaining stable. The sudden weather change was heralded by a spectacular sunset over Everest, the air washed clear so that everything seemed fresh and sharply focused. I hoped that at last this was a return to the normally stable, clear, cold weather common in the late autumn. As the evening shadows filled the valley, spilling up against the mountain walls, the withering sun fired the summit pyramid of Everest with a last defiant burst of colour until it glowed brightly above the surrounding peaks which lay in frozen shadows. I watched in wonder as it became a pyramid of beaten gold, rising majestically above the dark shadows falling away on all sides.

The lake at our base camp was a dirty brown, silted lozenge of glacial melt-water, half frozen and crazed into splintered webs of cracks, with scattered stones pitting the surface here and there. For a short time that evening it became a shimmering silver mirror with a perfectly symmetrical image of Everest and Nupste reflected in it. I watched as Ray, silhouetted against the silver lake, took photographs of the developing sunset.

Looking up at the summit ridge of Everest, I could just make out the distinctive notch of the South Summit and could guess where the slight nick of the Hillary Step formed just below the top. I remembered how, in 1991, I had stood by the same lake at mid-day and watched two Catalan climbers making their summit bid. Despite how I felt about the way some teams climbed the mountain the sight of those two tiny figures, invisible to the naked eye, tiny dots with barely perceptible limbs through my binoculars, gave me a rush of fear. They seemed so high, so very far away from help. I could see streamers of snow whipping through the notch at the South Summit and imagined how viciously cold it would have been. I was aware, that for the climbers, it would have been a completely different perspective, and that looking from my vantage point, humans appear remarkably insignificant.

The Catalans seemed to make painfully slow progress along the final part of the ridge. I found myself whispering exhortations as I peered through the binoculars, but another part of me was trying to yell to them to come down, get out of there and down to safety.

It was that empty, anxious, hungry sort of feeling that waiting for friends to return from a big climb is like, yet here were two strangers whom I had spotted only by chance. All the same, it was impossible to be unimpressed by a sight which made one feel vulnerable and concerned for them as well as exhilarated to witness the moment of their triumph. It was a strangely voyeuristic sensation, as if I were witness to some deadly serious gladiatorial contest with all at stake, and it was disturbingly addictive. Part of the excitement, I realised, was due to a vaguely disquieting worry about the very real danger they were in. Like watching a bull fight or a Formula 1 race, it was impossible to escape from the pervading thrill of what could happen at any moment. I suddenly understood why Eiger-watching had become such a grimly popular pastime in the late thirties and forties when so many climbers had perished in full sight of enthralled tourists peering through telescopes on hotel verandas in Grindelwald.

As the golden light began to seep away from the summit, bleeding into the advancing night sky, I headed back to the shelter of my tent. Pouring a shot of whisky into my tea, I zipped the door shut on the darkening mountains, thinking how different it must have been only five months before when a sudden unexpected storm had hit the summit ridge with tragic consequences. Eight died in that storm of 10 May 1996, bringing the total death toll on Everest (as far as we know) to 156 by the end of May 1997.

To date, a quite ghastly number of corpses have accumulated on or above the South Col. In 1993 at least five corpses were visible on the Col – three Nepalese, one Indian, and one Yugoslav. There were also two more Sherpas to be seen lying on the slopes above at 8400 metres. It was suggested that there may have been more as four Indian climbers had died and been left there in October 1985. By 1994 it was estimated that there were as many as nine bodies on or near the Col. There is something disturbing about these frozen corpses, and there is nothing noble about the way they have been abandoned. They are not mute, poignant testimony to an enduring spirit of adventure; they are simply the losers, abandoned by the winners.

Bodies have been left on mountains all over the world. Because many of these bodies lie in inaccessible or extremely dangerous positions, they cannot be buried. But the South Col of Everest is not inaccessible. Corpses beside which people camp are not exactly hard to reach. It has been shown that, with care, it is not too dangerous to retrieve them from this spot nor too exhausting to attempt some form of burial.

The truth is that it is expedient not to do anything. Who wants to waste time, energy, and the vast amounts of money they have spent trying to climb the mountain on retrieving corpses? As we all know, expediency is the essence of convenience, and that's what helps you get up Everest.

On 22 April 1993, Pasang Lhamu became the 17th woman and the first Nepalese woman to climb Everest. She descended very slowly, taking five hours to reach the South Summit, where she was benighted and forced to bivouac with her companions, Pemba Norbu and Sonam Tshering Sherpa. The following morning Pemba left her companion and descended alone to the South Col to get oxygen supplies for Pasang. The weather worsened, and despite repeated attempts, no one could reach the stricken climbers. Pasang

Lhamu died, and in so doing became a national heroine.

Eighteen days later her body was found near the South Summit and lowered down to the South Col by a team of Russian climbers. It was then brought down to the base camp by a South-west Face Korean team. Whether a reward had been offered for the recovery of this national heroine, or Everest climbers had suddenly got an attack of the moralities, is not clear. She was eventually taken back to the capital Kathmandu for national mourning. The funeral rites at Swayambhunath were attended by thousands of Nepali citizens. Never before had a body been recovered from such a height on the mountain.

The Russians and the Koreans had proved the lie of expediency. Not only did they retrieve her body safely but they got it all the way back down to Kathmandu for cremation and last respects. What does that say about those who continue to climb in the full knowledge that they will be camping beside corpses? Not a great deal. When they do so, they cannot claim to be surprised. Odd, isn't it?

If you have spent mortgage-size amounts of money to climb a mountain, then perhaps respect for the dead does become a secondary concern. Would it be so bad to say, '*Well, damn it, he isn't going anywhere for a while so I may as well climb to the top and then do something about him when I get down again.*' And then, when you get back to the Col, you can always say, '*Hell, I'm so knackered; it would kill me if I tried to do anything for that poor guy now, but at least I thought about it.*' Yes, at least you did.

I have to ask: would you do that at home? If you came across a corpse lying stiff and lifeless at the foot of a rock climb, would you step over it, finish your climb, and then come down and do what you thought was necessary? Would you camp beside it, for God's sake? No – of course you wouldn't, and yes – I am stating the obvious, but only because it seems necessary to do so. Why is it acceptable to behave in such a manner on the South Col? What does it say about our motivation and our humanity? What does it say about mountaineering in the nineties?

Retrieving a corpse from the Col can be dangerous, and I

would never suggest that a life should be risked in an effort to bury or retrieve the dead. It is not absolutely necessary to do what the Sherpas did with Pasang Lhamu. Surely a body could eventually be dropped down the Lhotse face to the Khumbu glacier. It sounds a somewhat uncaring thing to do, but it would at least enable some form of crevasse burial on the glacier if the body hasn't already been buried in the fall. If my body were lying in a similar position, I would far rather some stranger came along and hefted me into the abyss than be left to be gawped at by fellow mountaineers for years to come. Failing that, shouldn't there be a concerted effort to cover the body with rocks? Or perhaps it could be moved to a rarely visited area of the Col? Is that not showing more respect than camping beside it or stepping over it on the way to the summit?

There have been a number of well documented clean-up expeditions to the mountain which have attempted to remove the huge accumulation of rubbish and climbing detritus from the Everest base camp, and as far up the mountain as the South Col. The new environmental controls are enforced by the Sagamartha Pollution Control Committee (SPCC). Every climber is now obliged to pay for expensive bonds which have ensured that base camps are now left in a far cleaner condition. At higher altitudes, however, there seem to be no regulations covering behaviour on the mountain. I was amused to read on a notice board in the SPCC office in Namche Bazaar that, of the three categories of waste, the one listed as 'Disposable' included paper, packaging, boxes, clothes, and bodies.

Since Pasang Lhamu, no bodies have been lowered from the South Col, although some have been recovered from the Western Cwm. In 1993 the British climbing magazine, *High Mountain Sports*, printed a shocking colour photograph of the South Col in a littered state. It had been taken by the Belgian climber Karl Huyberechts, not out of some macabre voyeurism, but from a sense of passionate outrage at the desecration of the mountain. The French mountaineer, Pierre Royer, published the photograph on Karl's behalf in an effort to draw attention to the problem and in the hope that he could mount an expedition to clean up the mountain.

Karl Huyberechts's double-page, wide-angle photograph is a shocking indictment of high altitude mountaineering and its motives. In the foreground, almost obscured, as if casually tossed aside, lies the body of a man wearing a red down suit, face down in the rubble. For as far as one can see, the bleak barren rocks of the Col are dotted with bright yellow oxygen bottles. Shredded tents, half-buried under drifts of ice-hard snow, with skeletal poles pointing bleakly at the sky, add splashes of colour to a dirty scene. It looks like a scene from a battlefield. 'But this was never a war!' Even as the thought occurred to me I was immediately struck by the idiocy of the analogy. Soldiers are renowned for their efforts to retrieve and bury their dead.

Pierre Royer disappeared two years later in the autumn of 1995 while on an ascent of Kangchenjunga with the great French climber, Benoît Chamoux. Chamoux was attempting to become the first Frenchman and the fourth person to complete all fourteen of the world's 8000-metre mountains behind Erhard Loretan, the great Swiss mountaineer, who that very day had succeeded in becoming the third person to achieve this feat after Reinhold Messner and Jerzy Kukuczka. Loretan reached the summit without oxygen in the company of his fellow countryman Jean Troillet, and they passed the French pair during their descent from the summit.

Royer had decided to turn back some two hundred metres from the top, but he never made it back down to the high camp where Loretan and Troillet spent the night. Meanwhile, Chamoux continued up until he was forced to bivouac only fifty metres short of his goal, hoping to reach the summit the next day. In his radio call to base camp the following morning he revealed that he had been severely weakened by the exposed night at such a high altitude. He asked for the whereabouts of Royer, who hadn't been seen, and said that he was abandoning his summit attempt. He disappeared early that morning while descending somewhere on the north side of the mountain.

There have been calls for a complete ban on climbing Everest, citing the quite plausible argument that there is nothing left to be proved by an ascent other than to massage the egos of rich clients whose motives leave a lot to be desired. Sagamartha, 'Mother of the Universe', as the Sherpas call Mount Everest, or Chomolungma, 'Goddess Mother of the Wind', as she is known to the Tibetans, is now no more than 'an old whore made sordid and debauched by her clientele', according to Jim Crumley, the author of *Among Mountains*. Looking at Huyberechts's photograph of the South Col, I felt that Crumley might well have a point when he wrote in the *New Statesman* that: 'Ego massage for the rich is not justification enough for what Everest climbing has become. Pissing in the fair face of the Goddess Mother is not a noble human activity.'

His was perhaps the most extreme view I have heard voiced about the state of the mountain, and I am tempted to applaud him for saying what he did. At the same time, a logical extension of his argument would have all mountaineering cease. I cannot go along with that, but I can sympathise with Crumley's view that it is time for Everest to be made inviolate, closed to all suitors for all time, to become a sanctuary to be honoured, admired and respected rather than abused for profit and ego.

Ascents of Everest are by no means representative of the state of all modern mountaineering. Climbing today has reached the most extraordinary standards of technical excellence and outstanding ascents requiring incredible levels of skill, nerve, and adventurous commitment are being made all over the world, from wind-lashed Patagonian granite walls to frozen Alaskan ice-giants. Climbers have pushed the standards of rock and ice climbing to remarkable heights, and these skills have been carried forward into mountaineering. The leading mountaineers today tend to be experts in all fields of climbing in a way that was not the case twenty years ago. As a consequence, the difficulty, speed and style of ascents have reached levels undreamed of by those climbers on their cumbersome siege expeditions to the great Himalayan mountains in the mid-seventies. The vast south and south-west faces of Annapurna and Everest have now been climbed in Alpine-style in a matter of days rather than sieged over a period of months.

While Jim Crumley reasoned that it was time to bring to bear the wise philosophy of conservation on a mountain crying out for respect and sanctity, he rightly overruled any temptation to argue that expeditions provide vital economic resources for an impoverished nation. Trekkers would still come in their droves to view an 'Everest made sacred again.' Such economic arguments are as deceptively facile as saying that the sex industry that flourishes for Westerners visiting Thailand and the Philippines is justified because it provides a significant contribution to the economies of those nations.

'It will take the marshalling of world opinion,' Crumley writes, 'but to restore Everest's sanctity should be as high a priority of nature conservation as saving the tiger.' If he is correct, then it is a frightening analogy, given that the tiger, despite all international efforts at conservation, is today on the verge of extinction.

9

Second Guessing

I opened one eye and peered out of the small opening in my sleeping bag. A cloud of icy vapour drifted past, accompanied by a loud snore from my left-hand side. The massive bulk of Everest was just about visible as a dark forbidding mass looming in the night sky directly in front of me. A few stars twinkled in breaks in the thin cloud cover and a diaphanous moon leaked a weak silver wash across the white-laced ridges of the mountains. Another resonant snore rumbled into the night with its vapour cloud drifting past and the disturbing follow up sound of a man choking on a large frog. I kicked back with my heels and the frog seemed to escape with a sudden explosive cough and a sleepy grumble. It was some time yet until sunrise.

I tried twisting my lower torso into a more comfortable position but I seemed to have slipped into a narrow slot in the platform I had hastily constructed the previous night and was now jammed. A sharp and icy cold lump dug into my kidneys. I made a convulsive movement, throwing my sausage-shaped body to the side, and found myself just as restricted but now lying sideways in the slot, only partly on my sleeping mat. A snuffling noise announced the recurrence of the snoring which quickly grew louder. Ray had chosen the comfortable spot to one side and was braced against the small chorten someone had built near the summit cairn. Clearly he was enjoying his sleep.

The previous evening we had left base camp and strolled across to the small settlement of Gorak Shep with the intention of climbing Kala Patar before nightfall. This 5545-metre rock outcrop projecting from Pumori's South-west Ridge was a popular goal of trekkers who seemed to regard it as an independent summit on their Everest base camp itinerary. It certainly offered quite stunning views of the surrounding peaks. We had decided to copy Sandy Allen's idea of sleeping on the top to gain valuable acclimatisation but miscalculated how long the climb would take. So, after a couple of enforced beers at the small lodge in Gorak Shep, we found ourselves rapidly overtaken by darkness before getting halfway up the broad footpath made by thousands of previous trekkers. Having stumbled around in the dark for more than an hour, too lazy to get our head torches out, we finally reached the rocky spike on the ridge that was designated the summit of Kala Patar. I slumped down on to a plinth of rock, breathing heavily.

'It's amazing how a few beers can go to your head when you haven't drunk for a while.'

'I know. I thought we'd never get here,' Ray said mournfully as he delved into his rucksack for his torch. 'Nearly gave up at one point.'

I laughed. 'That would have been impressive. The Pumori South Buttress Expedition, or what's left of it, fails to climb Kala Patar.'

'What about a sleeping platform?' Ray asked, shining his torch beam around us. 'Seen anything?'

'This is about as good as it gets,' I said, nodding at the plinth that was gently angled downhill. A chorten the size of a small chimney stood at the foot of the slope, with a few desiccated prayer flags hanging limply from its top. 'That should stop us sliding off,' I added, pointing to the chorten.

'Do you think they'll mind?'

'Who?'

'The gods,' he said, shining his torch on the prayer flags.

'I shouldn't think so. It's not a proper memorial chorten, is it?' I said. 'It was probably built just to hold the string of flags in a line from the summit.'

'It's a bit cramped,' Ray muttered, almost to himself.

'Yeah but there're enough flat rocks around to extend it,' I said confidently.

An hour of heavy breathing and high altitude rock

12. Late monsoon storms clearing the South Ridge (centre) of Singu Chulu in the Annapurna Sanctuary. (Photo: Alison Reynolds)

13. 1996 Pumori Expedition – top row: Bruce French, Tony Halliwell, Tom Richardson, Ray Delaney, Steve Hartland, Ric Potter, Joe Simpson; front row: Richard Haszko, Amrit, Karen Gurung. (Photo: Simpson Collection)

14. Serious hairstyles.
Sadhus at Pashupatinath,
Kathmandu.
(Photo: Simpson)

15, 16. *Below*: A painful
way to earn a living. The
Sadhu demonstrates the
strength of his vital organ.
(Photos: Simpson)

17. Silent sentinels – the line of chortens on the hillside above Gorak Shep.
(Photo: Simpson)

18. Ray Delaney load-carrying on Pumori, with Ama Dablam above him.
(Photo: Simpson)

19. Yaks leaving Pumori base camp after delivering their loads, with Nuptse behind. (Photo. Simpson)

20. Everest rises above Joe and Ray at Pumori base camp. (Photo: Ric Potter)

21. Tom Richardson's memorial stone for Ari Gunnarsson, who fell to his death on Pumori in 1991. (Photo: Simpson)

22. Joe on the summit of Kala Patar. (Photo: Ray Delaney)

23. *Above*: Storm clouds clearing from Pumori's South Face. (Photo: Simpson)

24. *Left*: Ray on the snow ridge above 'The Buttocks'. (Photo: Simpson)

25. *Above right*: Ray at the base of the 'Star Buttress'. (Photo: Simpson)

26. *Right*: Joe on the mixed ground on the second day. (Photo: Delaney)

26. Altitude sickness put an end to the climb, and a suffering Ray descends. (Photo: Simpson)

sculpture produced a bigger platform, still slanting downhill but with sharp bits added.

'Here you go,' Ray said after we had struggled into our sleeping bags.

'What is it?'

'Supper.' Half a salami fell through the open drawstring of my bag.

'Thanks, just what I was looking forward to,' I muttered as I began biting into the tough outer skin in order to peel it off. 'I wish we had brought the stove now. I could kill a coffee.'

'Here, have some water.' There was a rustle and then a sharp blow on the side of my head as Ray's water bottle bounced off it. 'I think this is going to be one of those nights.'

'A starlight sojourn amid moonlit mountains bathed . . .'

'Sleepless,' Ray interrupted.

He was right. Like the story of the princess and the pea, our crude rock platform seemed to poke through our sleeping mats whatever position one laid in. Towards dawn I succumbed to an hour of exhausted slumber only to be woken by a perforated kidney and Ray's stentorian snores. The sky had lightened to a pale washed out blue, graduating to inky black on the horizon. I lay on my side and watched the sky lighten over the summit pyramid of Everest. Suddenly a silver starburst of dawn light began to sparkle on the distant rim of the South Col. I fumbled in the depths of my bag for my camera and shuffled myself into a half-sitting position. Looking down the length of my ice-covered bag, I could see the faint outline of the path snaking up towards us from the lodges at Gorak Shep. Already a few small figures could be seen wending their way slowly up the track with plumes of steamy breath rising above them in the freezing morning air. A few in the darker depths of the valley still had their head torches on and formed a string of bobbing yellow beads, small snakes of fireflies coming up from the dark shadows.

'Oh, hello,' a woman's voice said in the cultured vowels of middle England. 'Have you been here long?'

My eyes popped open in surprise. I had dozed off, still holding my camera. I glanced hurriedly towards Everest. The sun still hadn't appeared, but the summit was back-lit by a blaze of light that formed a golden corona radiating from behind the mountains. I looked warily back at the woman. *Where had she come from and what did she mean about being here long*? I grunted something unintelligible and dug my knee into the side of Ray, hoping he might feel more like a conversation than I did.

'Morning,' he said cheerfully, rolling on to his side and revealing the profile of his nose poking from his sleeping bag. 'Did you enjoy the climb?'

'Yes, it was wonderful. Didn't you?'

'No, I really can't say I did,' Ray replied. 'Too much beer and no torch.'

'Beer? At this time of the morning?'

'No, last night,' I said, pulling open the drawstring and shrugging my shoulders out of the bag. 'We slept up here.'

'Really? How exciting,' the woman said, obviously wondering why we should do such a thing.

'Training,' Ray added mysteriously as he stood up so that his bag fell in a down doughnut at his feet. 'God, it's freezing.' Hurriedly he pulled it back up to his chin and looked round. 'Hey, look at Pumori.'

I turned and stared at the mountain. The great flare of sun bursting over the South Col had lit the entire South face of Pumori in a wash of golden colour.

'Isn't the light fantastic?' the woman said from the pointy summit twenty yards away. 'I suppose that's why you slept up here, to wait for the light.'

'No we're in training to climb that,' Ray said, pointing his camera at Pumori's imposing pyramid and trying to look nonchalant.

'Are you mountain climbers then?' the woman asked dubiously, fixing me with a critical gaze.

'I bloody hope so,' I muttered inaudibly under my breath.

'Sleeping can't be very good training,' she added somewhat sniffily.

'Actually, we were practising not sleeping,' I said testily, 'at least, I was.' I glanced meaningfully at Ray, who smiled cheerfully.

'It's to get used to the altitude,' Ray explained. 'So we can climb that thing without dying on the way up.'

'You know, climb high, sleep low, that sort of thing,' I added helpfully.

'You don't look like climbers,' she remarked, watching me hop clumsily around the plinth, trying to put a boot on.

'Ah yes, well, we will in a week or so, once the beard growth has come on a bit.'

When her partner arrived a few minutes later we had to go through the rigmarole of explaining what we were doing in more detail – where the line of our route went, how long it would take and whether it was difficult to sleep at night on the mountain. It turned out that the woman was a friend of a friend of mine in Colorado. It was odd meeting her in a place like this. They said they were on an extended world tour, which included getting married in England after visiting Thailand, their next port. Shivering in the sunless morning air, I had a sudden flashback of tropical sunshine above coral lagoons, sun-filled days spent on the tropical beaches of Phra Nang and Koh Phi Phi in southern Thailand the previous January. For a moment, I wished I were there instead of staring at the vast ice-draped buttresses and snow-laden slopes of Pumori's South face.

'Hey, look at that,' Ray said, pointing at the faint snow ridge that led up to Camp I on Pumori's normal route. 'Could be Richard and Bruce.' He handed me his binoculars. Two tiny figures were moving slowly up the fixed lines.

'Well, if it is, they've done damn well,' I said, lowering the binoculars and looking down towards the tents of our base camp. 'It'll be a height record for both of them.'

'Base camp was a height record for Bruce,' Ray pointed out tartly.

'True,' I said with a chuckle. 'Come on, let's get down. This sun is never going to arrive.'

Two hours later, after a diverting short cut that saw us comprehensively lost in the chaotic moraines surrounding our base camp, we sat in the sunshine outside the mess tent, watching a tiny lone figure climb quickly above Camp I. Richard Haszko and Ric Potter sat nearby, sipping tea and also watching the climber. The figures we had seen from Kala Patar were Tony and Steve.

'Did you hear about the second Japanese team?' Richard asked.

'No. Did they climb it?'

'You're kidding. They were worse than the first lot.' Richard snorted. 'They hardly got above advance base camp. They'd give your average incompetent a bad name.'

He went on to tell us how he had watched the arrival of a second Japanese team whose Sherpas had quickly pitched and stocked their tents at the site of advanced base camp before starting to give lessons to the Japanese climbers in how to jumar. In a period of some hours, they failed to get more than fifty metres up the fixed lines above the camp. Descriptions of them spinning over on the ropes, sliding backwards, and turning upside down were both hilarious and disturbing. Fortunately, so bad were they that there was not the remotest chance of them getting high enough to endanger their Sherpas. The team had simply thrown money in the right direction to purchase a permit and a good Sherpa team without any regard for climbing ability or experience. We were horrified at the risks to which the Sherpas were being exposed. Some of the other teams on the normal route would surely have intervened if the Japanese had managed to get any higher. I wondered how many Sherpas had died through being handicapped by incompetent clients such as these.

'Christ! Look at him move,' Richard said, pointing to the lone climber far above us. 'Is he one of ours?'

'Don't know . . . don't think so,' Ric Potter replied. 'Steve and Tony should be on their way down here after staying last night at Camp I.'

'He doesn't look so sure now,' Ray said, peering through his binoculars. 'He looks distinctly worried to me.'

The figure had stopped. There was something about his body posture that suggested anxiety. Above him there was a wide heavily laden bowl of snow. It looked subtly different from the surrounding snow slopes. I watched him make some hesitant moves to one side, stop, look around, and then quickly descend to where he had been before.

'He's not on a fixed rope any more, is he?' I said.

'No, either they weren't fixed by the Japs or they've been swept away,' Ray replied.

'I must say it looks pretty dodgy, doesn't it?'

'Yeah,' I whispered, hoping we were not about to witness a tragedy. 'It's quite late for him to be pushing on towards the col and the summit. Maybe he's just worried about the time.'

'Not from the way he's moving,' Ric said. 'He doesn't like the slope. Rope or no rope, he thinks the slope might go. You can tell.'

'Well, that's us stuffed then,' Richard snapped. 'What can we do now?'

'Hang on, it's not over yet. You never know, it could have a perfectly plausible explanation,' I said trying to be optimistic.

'Not very likely, is it? Not after all those warnings we had about the snow.' Richard looked thoroughly dejected. 'I suppose we could try a trekking peak.'

'Look, don't give up yet, there could be any number of reasons why he's retreating.' Richard gave me a disbelieving look.

An hour passed before we were relieved to see the lone figure turn back towards the safety of Camp I. Once he was clear of the suspicious looking bowl, he immediately began down climbing with quite astonishing speed. Later that afternoon Steve and Tony arrived back in base camp, pleased with their stay on the mountain but depressed by news they had learned from the solo climber we had been watching.

'That was Peter Habeler,' Steve Hartland said, looking impressed.

'No wonder he was so damn quick,' I said.

Peter Habeler and Reinhold Messner had been legendary climbers in the '70s and '80s, with some extraordinary speed ascents in the Alps, including the North Face of the Eiger in an astonishing ten hours when most parties spent two to three days on the route. In 1978 they made mountaineering history by becoming the first to climb Everest without the use of supplementary oxygen. They did have the support and logistical help of an Austrian expedition, but nevertheless it was a bold and visionary ascent at a time when many experts believed that climbing at such height without oxygen would be fatal. In those days, regions above eight thousand metres were called the 'death zones'.

Reinhold Messner, of course, went on to become the first man to climb all fourteen of the world's 8000-metre peaks, as well as making the truly ultimate ascent of Everest alone, unsupported and without oxygen, by a hybrid new route on the Tibetan side in August 1980 – a feat only equalled since by the British solo climber Alison Hargreaves.

'Not bad for forty-eight years old, eh?' Richard said.

'I couldn't move that fast when I was twenty,' Ray replied, 'let alone at nearly fifty.'

'Yes, well, he also had pretty bad news about this route,' Tony said.

'I thought as much.' Richard bowed his head, expecting the worst.

'He told us that when he got to the snowy bowl area, he decided it was too dangerous to cross,' Steve said. 'He made a few attempts, but he was sure it was about to avalanche. It's a big area.'

'I know,' I said. 'We were watching. He didn't look happy. What was it? Wind slab?'

'Yes, I think so. Obviously when the Japanese succeeded, conditions were different . . .'

'Probably didn't even notice,' Ray muttered. 'Too busy being dragged uphill by their Sherpas.'

'He said there were no ropes there. Probably swept away.'

'Yeah, but there is no sign of crown walls above the bowl to show that it has avalanched.'

'Well, either way, not having a rope wouldn't stop a climber of his skill. He said it was possible, but he obviously didn't like the odds.'

'So is that it?' Richard asked, looking askance. 'I mean, if he can't do it, that's the end for us.'

'Yeah, it stuffs our route as well,' Ray said, looking glumly at me. 'Unless we abseil the south face, which I don't fancy.'

'He did say he might have another go,' Steve added. 'He made today's push from advanced base camp this morning, so he was obviously motoring. He reckoned it might be okay to cross the bowl early in the morning, before sunrise.'

Ray and I took turns with the binoculars as we scanned the new line that Tat and Ric had proposed for us. With Tat out of it, and Ric barely recovered from his pulmonary oedema, we had been reduced to a two-man team. At least we had managed to carry all the necessary equipment to the foot of the huge pear-shaped buttress at the start of our route. We had plenty of food and gas, plus a tent, all the required ice screws and rock gear as well as two hundred metres of polypropylene fixed on the lower easy angled couloir which ran up alongside the pear buttress.

'I still think we shouldn't have used the fixed rope,' I said, handing the glasses over.

'What do you mean?' Ray exclaimed. 'It was you who fixed the bloody thing.'

'Well, I know,' I muttered. 'I just thought at the time that without Tat and Ric it might help us get a quick springboard on to the face. Now I think it's a bit of a cheat . . . '

'Ah, come off it,' Ray said. 'It's fixed over easy ground right at the bottom. It just helps us with the initial load-carrying. It feels like a dangerous place. The rest of the route is serious enough as it is without getting finicky about that short bit of rope.'

'Yeah, I suppose you're right,' I agreed. 'And it is a dodgy place. I doubt if that three-ply rope would hold much of a fall anyway. I'm not sure I'd tie a dinghy up with it myself. The way it crackles and goes hairy after abseiling on it gives me the creeps.'

'It's okay as a static line,' Ray retorted. 'But I know what you mean. Thin end of the wedge and all that nonsense . . . '

'Yeah, except it's not nonsense, is it?' I interrupted. 'If you're going to use two hundred metres of rope, why not use two thousand?'

'Hardly the same,' Ray said. 'At least we're making the effort to do it well. This is a small compromise.'

'I suppose our best bet would be to leave here tomorrow, pick up the food and hardware, and then climb as far as we can above the fixed ropes, and try to make a camp at the foot of that small buttress.'

'Which buttress?'

'The grey one above the couloir,' I said, pointing. 'It looks like a pair of buttocks, do you see?'

'Ah, right,' Ray said at last. 'And then what?'

'Camp beneath the right cheek. It looks sheltered there – and then climb the buttocks the next day leading to that second bigger star-shaped buttress.'

'Star shaped buttress?' Ray muttered as he searched the face. 'Ah there, I see it, and we can either take it on the left edge, although that looks a bit difficult to me, or else we can climb straight up the rock in the middle to reach the icefield above . . . '

'Then it's straight up that line of old seracs, and if we can break through that rock band by the couloir on the summit ridge, we can finish direct to the top.'

'If,' Ray said pointedly and rubbed his eyes with the heel of his palms. 'Have you seen the size of those guys on the normal route. They're tiny.'

'Yeah, it's a big face, well over a mile high. Makes it feel pretty committing, doesn't it?'

'Just a little.' We stared silently at the face, trying to work out all its weaknesses, which points had to be avoided, which was the best line of ascent or retreat. In its own way, this study of a mountain is an absorbing and deeply satisfying part of the whole process of climbing. On one level it is an essential way of getting thoroughly familiar with all aspects of the face so that, once on it in possibly bad conditions, we would always have a sense of where we were, a perspective of the whole geography of the face. It also helped to break down the mountain into constituent parts we could understand and deal with so that it no longer presented this massive and intimidating front.

As we carried loads up beneath the huge sweep of the face things began to fall into place. The route appeared very fore-shortened, but through constantly examining it with the binoculars we could recognise all the features we had named and firmly fixed in our minds. It was like a gradual psycho-logical adjustment, a process that enabled us to get our confidence together and go for the climb.

'What do you reckon?' I said, looking at Ray. 'Shall we do it?'

'Now is as good a time as any,' he said. 'The weather looks good, and if the conditions are okay, we have a chance.'

'How many days do you reckon we'll need?'

'At least five,' Ray said, counting off on his fingers. 'Tomorrow up to the stash and then on to the buttock camp, next day up the buttocks to camp at or above the star-shaped buttress. Next day, up the broken seracs to camp near the summit rock band. After that, up to the summit, then down to camp on the col on the normal route . . .'

'Or as low as their Camp I if we're lucky?'

'Yeah, that's possible. So what's that then? Four nights on the face and one on the descent – five days minimum.'

'Okay. We'll take food for five and fuel for six,' I said. 'A gas cartridge per day for the pair of us should be enough, with one spare.'

'Sounds okay,' Ray said with a grin. 'Tomorrow then?'

'Well, why not rest a few more days and see what happens with Habeler's second attempt,' I suggested. 'I'd feel better going for it if we knew that the descent was okay, and what the snow conditions were like near the summit.'

'Good point, I still don't fancy abseiling the face.'

Later that afternoon I ambled across to the site of the base camp we had occupied in 1991. It was on a crescent beach of fine mica sand at the southern tip of the lake. Behind it a jumbled pile of boulders formed a high ridge between the camp site and the nearby Khumbu glacier. The sand was scuffed with tracks and dotted here and there with yak dung. Once on the beach, I began searching for the memorial stone Tom had carved for Ari Gunnarsson. In the sea of massive boulders of all shapes and sizes I had no idea where to look. I spotted a couple of large plinth-like boulders with neatly piled rocks stacked on their tops, but when I reached them I found that they were only *puja* altars or pillars to support strings of prayer flags. I had decided to abandon the search when I spotted the stone silhouetted against the sunlit summit pyramid of Everest.

Though barely visible, I could just make out the deeply

etched grooves which lichen had long since colonised. It must have taken Tom a long time to carve the name into the flinty red granite slab. 'ARI GUNNARSSON. Pumori. 9:10:91' A small chorten had been erected on a huge flat-topped boulder. It stood a few feet high, lodged amidst a nest of interlocked stones.

I scrambled up on the boulder and sat beside the chorten for a moment, contemplating the view of the south face of Pumori, trying to remember what the young Icelander had been like. Already I could conjure up no more than scattered images of him. It happened only five years ago yet he had become no more than a familiar faded name on a sun-bleached tablet of stone. I remembered his typically Scandinavian blond hair, his Blues brothers style sun glasses and how, at Dugla, on the walk in, he had insisted that I should try his stock of dried cod and haddock. He'd shown Tom and I a photograph of his ten-year-old son holding a salmon almost as big as himself by the tail. We'd promised to visit him in Iceland. And that was all. It was amazing how quickly the memory of people withered with their loss. If they are no longer living, vital parts of our lives then they tend to fade from our memories. We quickly lose sense of their individual traits, the way they smiled, the turn of phrase they used, the look in their eyes. They become strangers. I wonder whether we are also able to alienate ourselves from strangers in the same way. Is that the mechanism by which we are capable of abandoning people to their fates? Is that how young men can be trained to be soldiers and kill for their country?

Although my memory of Ari had faded, I could recall all too clearly what happened to him and my own part in the expedition. It was perhaps foolish even to think of joining it with a broken ankle that had not healed since my fall on Pachermo. Doctors had wanted to fuse the joint, warning me against any further strain on my legs. They had suggested a similar cure for my right knee after the drama on Siula Grande if I wanted to walk normally again, and I had refused the irreversible remedy. Since that time I have been on fifteen mountaineering expeditions, and felt vindicated enough to test the strength of the ankle by crutching into Pumori in

1991. I will not forget the pain of that walk-in, but I have let Ari slip from my memory.

In the end I was forced to abandon the climb at 6200 metres, leaving Mal and Liz Duff and Mark Warham to complete a successful ascent while I followed their progress through binoculars at base camp. Tom Richardson, who had been delayed joining our expedition, arrived in time to watch with me as the three topped out on the normal route.

I left base camp early and hobbled furiously back to the airport at Lukla. The next day Ari Gunnarsson was killed by falling ice only minutes from the safety of Camp I. Ari had told me that he wanted to climb the mountain as a memorial to the death of two Icelandic friends who had been killed in an avalanche while descending from the summit. It hadn't seemed a good reason to climb anything.

There was a strange twist to Ari's death. When he set out from Camp I to make his quick solo dash to the summit and back in a day, he elected to leave several items of equipment behind – ostensibly, we later guessed, to save weight. He left his helmet, his harness, and the wrist loop for his ice axe in the tent. Even stranger for a solo climber, he left behind his compact lightweight camera. Few climbers would set out for the summit of such a beautiful mountain in an area as spectacular as the Khumbu without a camera to record the climb. From Pumori the views of Everest, Nuptse, Lhotse, and far behind, Makalu, are truly fabulous.

On a mountain which is so threatened by objective dangers, I find it inconceivable that anyone would set off without a helmet. Without a harness that weighs less than half a pound, Ari would have had to rely entirely on his hand strength to hold on to the jumar when ascending some of the fixed ropes on the upper slope, and would not have had the added security of being able to abseil down again.

When he had descended from the summit to a point only a few minutes from the safety of the snow spur on which Camp I was situated, he chose to stop for a drink of water at a very exposed spot. The slopes above this camp are lined with a series of ice cliffs and seracs that threaten the area at all times of the day. In fact, earlier in the trip, Mal Duff had very nearly been killed by an ice avalanche as he reconnoitred the slopes leading towards the north-east ridge. Luckily he found a small hole into which he could dive to avoid the scatter gun effect of the ice debris that swept harmlessly past.

Ari was not so lucky. A German climber, descending a hundred metres above him, witnessed Ari receive a blow on his temple from a half-brick size lump of ice that had fallen from the seracs over a thousand feet above him. The blow to his unprotected head was sufficiently hard to knock him unconscious and he fell, stunned, on to a relatively easy-angled ice slope, dropping his ice axe as he did so.

While the axe remained where it fell, Ari began to slide down very slowly. The German climber saw him regain consciousness as the slope became steeper where it approached the top of a thousand-foot drop to the glacier. Without an axe, his bare-fingered attempts to brake were futile, and he plunged down a steep couloir to the east of Camp I. The German climber who recovered the axe felt sure it would have been a relatively easy slide to stop. If he had kept his wrist loop, a weight-saving of a few ounces, it would have spared his life.

Perhaps Ari wasn't a very experienced climber, or hadn't been thinking clearly that day. Of course, all these mistakes were discovered after the event, and presumably if Ari had not been hit by that stray lump of ice, no one would have been critical of him. Apart from finding his harness, wrist loop, helmet and camera in Camp I after the accident, Mal also made the strange discovery that among Ari's remaining possessions he had no money – no travellers cheques, foreign currency or credit cards, in fact no money whatever, and he would have needed some for the walk out to Kathmandu. Unless he took it all with him, which is highly unlikely, this last discovery remains inexplicable.

Poor Tom, who had been at the base camp for little more than 36 hours, found himself going up to advance camp with Mal in the desperate hope of finding Ari alive. He had fallen out of sight into a steep couloir line and there was just the merest chance that he may have survived and be lying injured on the mountain. Darkness fell before a thorough search could be made, and during the night a huge ice avalanche exploded down the couloir. Next morning Tom and Mal were faced with the grisly task of having to locate and recover the body.

Tom was the first to spot Ari's remains, but they were scattered over such a dangerous area that all hopes of retrieving him for burial were abandoned. The slopes were threatened throughout by another collapse of the seracs hanging above Tom and Mal. They had risked their lives in the hope of finding Ari alive and any further risk was now unjustified. Before leaving, Tom spent hours painstakingly carving a stone memorial plaque for a man he had known for less than two days. He mounted the engraved slab of granite on a plinth of smaller rocks with the black summit of Everest as a backdrop. It wasn't much of a memorial either to Ari or his two Icelandic friends.

Five years later, I lifted the carved slab carefully from its setting and laid it gently on the boulder. Having collected some sharp-sided stones, and also using a tent peg I had brought with me, I traced around the letters, rubbing the lichens away so that the whitened lettering stood out clearly. I knew it wouldn't last long. I had vainly searched base camp for some suitable paint, ink or marker pen that might have been more permanent. It was pleasant to sit in the sun, absorbed in a task, feeling the heat on my back. Occasionally the great roar of an avalanche on Nuptse, or the distant rumble of a serac collapse, broke the afternoon silence, and I would look up at the mountains and try to spot the tell-tale puff clouds of pulverised ice crystals. When I had finished, I replaced the slab and stuffed a handful of juniper that I had taken from our *puja* altar into a small square opening in the face of the chorten. At the first touch of the match it burst into flames, invisible in the fierce brightness of the sun, and a fragrant cloud of smoke drifted up and over the carved slab.

As I turned to descend to the beach I was surprised to see a group of Europeans gathered round a pile of barrels and kit-bags at the water's edge. It was a French team, led by the superb mountaineer Jean Christophe Lafaille. They had just arrived to make an attempt on the normal route. I had heard about some of Lafaille's incredible exploits, including a recent solo attempt of the British route on Annapurna, a bold attempt considering his previous experience on the mountain. In 1993, he had reached 7300 metres with Pierre Béghin on the central couloir of the South Face before they were forced to retreat in bad weather. During the descent, he witnessed his friend fall to his death when the abseil anchor failed and Lafaille was forced to solo down climb the rest of the route despite sustaining a broken arm in a near fatal rock fall. He was a diminutive figure, dwarfed by his companions, but he proved to be a friendly and approachable man despite his 'star' status in French climbing circles. As I returned to our tents I couldn't help thinking about the contrast between climbers such as Habeler and Lafaille and the incompetent group of Japanese being taught how to jumar by their Sherpas.

Several days of fine weather passed. Richard and Bruce succeeded in reaching their high point at Camp I (6200m), returning with news of Habeler's second attempt on the face. We had watched him swiftly descending from the col on the North-east Ridge after overcoming the problem of the windslab section. He had reached a point one hundred metres below the summit only to be forced back by chest-deep powder snow. It had been an impressively fast effort, taking little more than nine hours to climb from base camp almost to the summit and down again. Most teams took at least two and a half days to accomplish as much.

Habeler reported that conditions up to his high point were reasonably good but the powder snow was an ominous revelation. Ray and I nevertheless decided that we would make our attempt the next day, 2 November.

That evening, as I retreated to my sleeping bag, I saw the great plume of ice extending from Everest's summit ridge. The jet stream winds had already come in low enough to begin the winter cycle of stripping away the monsoon snow. I felt pessimistic about our chances of success. So many things had gone wrong, what with Ric and Tat getting sick, and the worrying reports about avalanche conditions, that it had begun to erode my self confidence, despite feeling as fit and strong as I had for years. We had worked so hard to organise this expedition. As usual, Ray was quite laid back about things. He felt that at least we should go up and see what it was like, get some 'face time' in, as he put it, climb some unclimbed territory, take things from day to day. For my part I was just as anxious to get away from the inertia of base camp life and spend time on the hill with Ray, just the pair of us moving together in our own world, answerable to no one, responsible entirely for ourselves.

10

Face to Face

'Let's not hang around,' Ray said as he bent over to fasten his crampons. 'I don't like this place. There's been too much melting.'

I looked up from where I sat on some dry scree. Behind Ray a huge cave, hollowed from the edge of the glacier, seemed to hover over us. A great fringe of blue icicles hung in splay-fingered fronds, pointing menacingly at the track we had just hurried along from the dump site. Some large chunks of blue ice, speckled with grit, lay scattered across the faint tracks we had made on earlier load-carrying trips. I could see where these weighty ice bombs had fallen from clean, fresh fracture points in the ice cave.

'I know, it gives me the creeps,' I said, picking up my axe and struggling to my feet under the weight of my heavily laden rucksack. 'The whole thing could go all at once.'

The scraping sound of crampon points drew my attention back to Ray who was quickly front-pointing up a short sixty-five degree ice wall. A fringe of precariously balanced boulders protruded over the top edge of it. I stepped up on to the ice and followed as fast as I could, anxious to put distance between myself and the fragile ice cave. Ten minutes later we were both safely established on the glacier, having climbed up through a maze of small crevasses and tottering boulders. Ray heaved his rucksack from his shoulder and dropped it at his feet. A small flurry of scree sprayed away down an adjoining fissure. The stones made hollow echoing clicks and thumps as they disappeared into the depths.

'What are you doing?' I demanded. 'We've only just started.'

'Photo time,' Ray replied, and aimed his camera at me. 'Anyway, we're in no rush. It should only take two or three hours to reach the base of the buttocks, which means we'll still be in the sun to dig our tent platform.'

'Yeah, well, I was thinking that, if we have time, we should climb up the buttress above the camp and leave our lead ropes fixed for the morning.'

'Seems a good idea.' Ray put away his camera. 'God, it's good to be on the hill at last after all that hassle.'

'The weather looks settled enough.'

'Come on, let's do it.'

At the foot of a huge sweep of grey granite that formed the pear buttress I found the end of the thin white polypropylene rope I had fixed in place over a week before. Where previously the entire slope had been blanketed in heavy and somewhat worrying deep wet snow, there was now a considerable amount of rock showing. The freezing night-time temperatures had consolidated my old footprints into solidly carved steps, and so progress was fast and easy. For the most part, I simply pulled hand over hand up the rope, using it for balance, until the angle reared up steeply near the top of the buttress.

I stopped to look down between my legs at Ray taking a breather, head bent forward over his ice axe. All the way down the slope there were dark stains of rock dust and debris and the occasional large stone. There was a cracking sound from above and to my right. I looked round quickly, hunching my shoulders in anticipation of an impact. Nothing came down. I looked down again at Ray and then up the impending granite wall that loomed over him. In places, I could see that the rock face was heavily fractured.

'I wouldn't hang around,' I shouted. 'There's been a lot of rock fall here.'

He lifted his arm in acknowledgement, and I turned and continued up the slope, trying to keep close in against the rock wall in the hope that falling stones would fly safely out and over my head. The snow gradually deteriorated, eventually becoming dry, grit-covered ice, blackened by age and rock dust. A rivulet of muddy water streamed over the surface. On my left a natural cave offered shelter, so I edged across the ice and rested there for a moment. The white three-stranded rope flapped against the ice as Ray pulled up on it from below. I examined the rope for hairy marks and lumps on the fibres that would show where it had been hit. Five feet above me I could see where one of the strands had been cleanly cut through. I gingerly moved up to examine the lacerated section and was glad to find that the remaining two strands were undamaged. Looking down, I saw that Ray too had stopped. I indicated the cut rope and made a chopping motion with the side of my hand, I then gave a thumbs up sign. He nodded his head. As I set off above the cut I wondered whether he had understood my warning, or if he had just taken it as a friendly enquiry as to whether he was okay.

Two hundred metres of climbing led to a narrowing where a serac band pinched against the walls of the buttress. A week earlier it had been a smooth gully of compacted snow but now it was rock-hard black ice, scoured by deep grooves and water worn fissures. Sparks flickered from the pick of my axe as I struck rocks embedded in the ice and I found myself teetering on the tips of my crampon points. Ray was framed between my legs three hundred feet below me. I moved carefully from pick placement to crampon kick, trying to avoid the loose rocks that had been left high and dry on tiny ice pedestals as the snow had melted away. After a few more tentative moves I found myself on easier ground, back on snow again as the slope above the funnel between the seracs opened into a small diamond-shaped snowfield.

Half an hour later I sat in a natural hollow at the left side of what we had dubbed The Buttocks, a two-hundred-foot high rock buttress which was cleaved into two distinct curving cheeks at its base. A shallow gully chock full of loose boulders and stacked layers of frost-shattered tiles of rock, formed the divide between the cheeks. I examined it carefully while Ray climbed the last rope length to the hollow. Anything falling down the gully would bounce and fall leftwards away from the site of our proposed tent platform. At the far end of the hollow a natural bulge in the rock provided a safe shield against the possibility of ice or loose rocks falling directly from above. Even a large avalanche would be divided by the buttress and leave the tent unscathed.

'That didn't take long, did it?' Ray said, as he clipped into the belay I had set up.

'No, and the buttress doesn't look too bad either,' I responded, feeling a sudden surge of enthusiasm and building confidence. 'This might work, you know.'

'Just what I was thinking.' Ray's smile was infectious. We had both felt constrained at base camp, and I had been very wound up over the past few weeks while organising the trip and dealing with all the bureaucratic hassle that went with it. Dire warnings by everyone we met along the way that we would all be buried in monster avalanches hadn't helped morale. With Ric and Tat falling sick, and losing most of our kitchen staff as well as our Sirdar, I had begun to feel as if a dark cloud had fallen over the whole Pumori enterprise. Calm objective diplomacy and fair-minded patience had never been my strong suit, so I probably wasn't best equipped to be the leader.

Yet, once away from the idle tensions at base camp (most of them created by me, as Ray so kindly pointed out), we felt suddenly released and our excitement came flooding back.

'Let's have a go at the buttress while the sun's still on it,' I said as I uncoiled one of the lead ropes.

'Okay.' Ray dumped his sack on the hollowed-out ledge. 'You lead. I'll have a rest. You should be able to belay up there at the Builders bum,' he said, pointing at where the narrow cleft dividing the buttress pinched shut a rope length above us.

The rock climbing proved to be fairly straightforward. The first rope-length consisted of steep granite corners and short walls interspersed with ledges that led to a more broken area where I managed to fix a belay. Ray quickly joined me and we looked down at the glacier we had climbed that morning. It lay in shadows that were inexorably creeping across the valley floor. The brown lake was free of ice, and we could just make out the blue colour of the mess tent nestling amid huge boulders nearly a thousand feet below us.

'Quite a view,' Ray said, staring towards Everest with the snaking chaotic moraines of the Khumbu glacier dominating the valley. 'That looks like death on a stick,' he said, nodding at the Khumbu ice fall which guarded access to the Western Cwm.

'I know,' I agreed. 'It's almost impossible to work out which way they take through it.'

'But you can see right up the Cwm, can't you?' he said. 'The whole of the Lhotse Face, the Geneva Spur, the South Col and the South-east Ridge are visible. No wonder Eric Shipton got so excited.'

'Wasn't it Shipton who said "for God's sake climb the wretched thing and let us get back to real mountaineering"?'

'He was certainly the one who led the reconnaissance team up here in 1951 and found that it was feasible to climb Everest from Nepal.'

'No, wait a minute, it wasn't Shipton but a friend of his who said it after the Everest expeditions in the thirties,' I said. 'Still, Shipton was pretty caustic about the huge expeditions of those days. Didn't like them at all.'

Eric Shipton and Bill Tilman were extraordinary mountaineers and explorers whose exploits in the Karakoram and Himalayas are renowned. Tilman's ascent of Nanda Devi with Odell in 1936 was hailed as an incredible achievement. They frequently travelled on shoe-string budgets climbing as two-man teams using the minimum of porters and equipment and always climbing Alpine-style. In the same mould as Whymper and Mummery, they became legendary figures in the history of British mountaineering.

'You know, Shipton thought that the cult of the mighty Himalayan campaigns had a terrible effect on high altitude mountaineering. He often complained that it made everyone think that only huge numbers of climbers and vast sums of money would lead to success.'

'Not much has changed then,' Ray said, as he looked at me and laughed.

I gazed across at the Everest summit bathed in late afternoon sun. The Western Cwm now lay in shadow, icy and uninviting. 'George Mallory saw into the Western Cwm, you know.'

'Did he? But I thought all his attempts were made on the Tibetan side?'

'Yeah, but early on, in 1921 I think, he climbed to a col between Lingtren over there and the end of Pumori's north-east ridge, so he *must* have seen the entire southern route as well. He dismissed it as impossible, cold and forbidding, which shows how wrong you can be.'

'Surely Nepal was out of bounds to climbers then,' Ray pointed out, 'so whether there was a climbable route on the south side or not was academic.'

With a heavy reverberating thunder, a plume of ice particles suddenly erupted from the centre of the Khumbu Icefall.

'Bloody hell, that must be big!'

We were well over a mile from the collapse and yet the sound was tremendous. I looked at the billowing white cloud and wondered what it would be like to climb through such a dangerous icefall. Towers of ice weighing hundreds, if not thousands of tons, must have thundered down to create a blast of such force, yet, from this distance, it looked no more than a puff of downy soft cloud.

'Did you know that Shipton and the reconnaissance team actually succeeded in climbing the Khumbu Icefall?' I said. 'There were only about six of them and they climbed it in five days. They had no Sherpa team with them either. They would have reached the Western Cwm but for one huge crevasse above the Khumbu Icefall.'

'And I thought they had only spotted the route from Pumori.'

'Shipton could never have imagined how wrong his friend would be about "real" climbing.'

'They were years ahead of their time, you know. Tilman was always going on about the "unattainable ideal" of lightweight climbing long before the term "Alpine-style" had been invented. Instead we got siege tactics and the false security of safety in numbers.'

'You can see why,' Ray muttered, looking down on our tiny distant base camp. 'It can feel a bit lonely up here.'

'Rubbish! It's grand, the sun is shining and we have it to ourselves,' I said and clipped my belay plate into the rope. 'And it's your lead. Off you go.'

An hour later Ray slid down his lead rope and rejoined me at the stance.

'I've tied it off at those rocks up there on the left,' he said, pointing to a sharp spike of rock protruding from the top of the buttress. 'I only used about half the rope length because I ended up on a snow ridge.'

'Took your time, didn't you?' I said, grinning at his expression of dismay.

'It took me ages to find an anchor,' he protested, 'and even then it's only a couple of dodgy wires and a moving rock spike.'

'I was only kidding.' I pressed his shoulder. 'Look, why don't you abseil down and start digging out the tent platform? I'll pull up these ropes and run the remainder out up the ridge if it looks safe.'

'All right. See you shortly,' he said, clipping his figure of eight to the lower rope. 'Be careful.'

'I will – and stop calling me "shortly",' I yelled after his dwindling figure.

The sun was holding tenaciously to the upper slopes of the mountain as I reached Ray's high point but I could see a blue frontal wave of shadow edging towards me on the face below. Already Ray was in shadow. I saw him bent forward, swinging rhythmically with his axe at the hard snow by the foot of the buttress. Above me, an open slope ran up to a snow ridge that formed a temporary horizon. A black spike of rock, one side catching the gold of the sun, protruded above the knife-sharp white ridge. I guessed that with the extra rope I had gained by straightening the line and with a bit of judicious rope joining, I might be able to reach the rock. The open slope to my left had formed into a series of frozen slates like icy roof tiles jutting out at forty-five degrees.

I stepped gingerly to my left, kicking the toe of my boot hard in between two snow spikes, and driving the shaft of my ice axe deeply into the slope. Soon I was absorbed in the task of soloing up the slope, taking care because I wasn't wearing crampons but delighting in the solitude and beauty of the position.

Every now and then I stopped to catch my breath and

looked across at Everest, Lhotse and Nuptse and felt a great surge of joy coursing through me, just from being there, alone, with the mountain to myself. I could feel all the stress and aggression of the past few weeks melting away. The shadows came casting up the slope, racing my heels in a dark blue line up the serried ranks of *penitentes* as a wave sweeps up a corrugated sandy beach.

Glancing up, I was delighted to see the rock spike just off to my right and slightly lower on the crest of the ridge. After a few crabbed sideways steps, leaning against the insistent stretch of the rope, I got one arm around the spike and quickly draped a large sling over it. In the few minutes it took to tie off the rope safely and organise myself for the abseil the sun had gone down, and with it the temperature plummeted.

I shivered as I slid quickly down to the top of the first pitch. A thin, lightly insulated windproof wasn't enough to fight the cutting cold of early November. Far below me, I saw Ray pulling a duvet jacket on to his arm. A splash of sky blue showed that he had pulled out the tiny two-man single skinned Mountain Gemini tent that we had brought with us.

'That was brilliant,' I yelled across at Ray as I unclipped at the bottom of our lead ropes. 'The snow was fantastic. This is going to work you know. It really is.'

'Keep your knickers on,' Ray said, looking tired, 'and come and do some digging, you lazy sod.'

'Did you bring the shovel?'

'Yeah, but it's a bit icy,' Ray replied. 'You'll need your axe as well. I've done most of it, but the ledge needs to be wider.'

An hour of hacking at blue water ice eventually produced a scoop-shaped ledge large enough to accommodate the tent. Ray, a considerably bigger man than I am, sorted out his equipment first and then eased himself into the narrow cramped tent. There was no zipped porch on the front but a clever design feature meant that a long extended tube of material protruding from the rear of the tent could be stuffed full of rucksacks, boots and helmets to provide the maximum amount of space inside the tent. It was a calm evening without a breath of wind, so I was able to set up the stove in a sheltered hole in the ice in front of the doorway. A great pile of ice chippings from which to brew drinks had been heaped to the side of the door. I arranged my sleeping mat and bag so that my head would be at the door end of the tent as I had chosen to be the brew-master for the climb. It was something I always preferred doing since I found it almost impossible to sit idly by and watch someone else cooking and producing hot drinks. I was always convinced that my way of doing it was more efficient or quicker, which was probably untrue, but I found it a torture to sit and watch someone else doing it in a completely different way. Ray seemed pretty content to leave it all to me and lay back on the downy mound of his sleeping bag and cat-napped as I worked.

Spinach soup, sliced salami, combined with reheated dahl baht from Amrit's kitchen was washed down with several litres of sweet tea, each followed by a pudding of a high carbohydrate energy bar.

'I feel sick,' Ray murmured from the back of the tent when we had finished eating. He groaned loudly.

'I know,' I agreed, 'why does it always taste so weird?'

'Altitude.' A loud belch erupted from behind me and a pair of socks appeared at my shoulder.

'God, your feet stink.'

'Thank you,' Ray said. 'Kind of you to notice. Anything else interesting to add?'

'The weather looks good,' I said, peering out of the open door over the hissing gas stove. 'Should be a freezing night.'

'Good.' Ray leant forward and pushed his head over my shoulder. 'Bruce should have another chilly night.'

'Bruce?'

'Yeah, up there.' Ray nodded at Everest, 'Somewhere.'

'Ah, that Bruce. Well, he shouldn't be there, should he?'

'No, I don't think so.' Ray shook his head. 'I knew him you know?'

'Yeah, you said.'

'I mean I didn't know him really well,' Ray added, 'but I liked him. I was pretty surprised to hear that he was even going to Everest, let alone find out that he was making a summit bid. He was a photographer more than a climber, a good one at that.'

'Was he experienced enough to go for Everest then?' I asked.

'I wouldn't have thought so.' Ray shrugged. 'But who knows now? Everyone and his grandmother seems to climb it nowadays – doesn't matter how much they've done. If they can afford the price, they're in. It's stupid . . .'

The water came to the boil and I busied myself with making the last brews of the night and filling our water bottles. I lay on my side, propped on one elbow, watching Everest turn varying shades of gold. She did it almost every night, and we took it for granted after a while. I could see the slight bump of the South Summit and thought about Ray's friend, Bruce Herrod, who had been with the South African team on the South Col route the previous spring. After the disastrous storm that had claimed so many lives there were several more ascents from the Nepalese side. On 23 May David Breashears led the IMAX film expedition on his third ascent, accompanied by Ed Viesturs (fourth ascent), Robert Schauer (second ascent) , and Araceli Segarra, making the first ascent by a Spanish woman. They were shortly followed by the extraordinary cycling Swede, Göran Kropp, who, it was reported, avoided using not only the fixed ropes but even most of the existing tracks – a real purist of a mountaineer.

Two days later Ian Woodall, the man whom we had guided up Island Peak in 1990, and who was now leader of the South African team, made a summit bid with Cathy O'Dowd, Bruce Herrod, and three climbing Sherpas. Five of the six climbers left the South Col at around midnight; Bruce Herrod was delayed and left a little later. Ian Woodall reached the summit with Pema Tengi just before ten o'clock in the morning and was soon joined by a lone Cathy. It was a fast ascent, albeit ably assisted by the ropes and well trodden tracks left by all the previous expeditions.

An hour and a half later the other two Sherpas arrived at the top after the three summiters had started their descent. Bruce Herrod, in the meantime, had been making steady if extremely slow progress on his own and was passed by the descending Woodall and O'Dowd. For some odd reason, Woodall thought that Herrod was making good progress and that, since the weather was perfect, there was no reason to turn their companion back, despite the fact that Bruce had taken nearly thirteen hours to reach the South Summit and it was already very late in the day. It is notoriously difficult for any leader to turn back a determined team member once a summit bid has started, and in truth everyone is responsible for themselves, but to admit that they saw no reason to say anything to him seems quite extraordinary.

So late in the day was it that Bruce Herrod didn't reach the summit until five o'clock in the afternoon. He radioed Woodall, to tell him of his success, and was also patched through base camp to his friend Sue Thompson in London via a satellite phone link. In his high spirited radio conversation with Woodall, they agreed that he would radio again from the end of the fixed ropes near the South Col so that his companions could come out to find him. He was never heard from again. Woodall could only assume that he had slipped and fallen some time during the descent. If he had succumbed to the cold or exhaustion, he would surely have attempted to communicate with them on his radio. Arriving at the summit by the time darkness was imminent does not seem to be the act of an experienced climber who is thinking clearly. That his colleagues should display an equally blasé attitude to the late hour and the seriousness of the situation suggests that they had learned precious little from recent events.

In 1993, when a total of 129 climbers got to the summit of Everest (40 of them in a single day), a furore erupted over the excessive numbers allowed on the mountain at one time. Reports spoke of congestion and delays on the summit ridge, and warned that such a situation would inevitably lead to a disaster in the future. Negative media coverage and complaints from various international mountaineering bodies led to the Nepalese government being urged to change its peak permit rules. Only one team was to be allowed on a route in any one season, and a large increase in the cost of a permit (from $10,000 to $50,000) was imposed as a deterrent. Four years later the authorities relaxed these rules and allowed twelve expedition permits for the Everest South Col route in the spring season, and unfortunately disaster struck. Even a surcharge of $20,000 for teams wishing to attempt the South Col route had no effect on the mountain's popularity. It appears that the Nepalese Ministry of Tourism paid little heed to the complaints and warnings about the dangers of 'climbing gridlock' above eight thousand metres. It did create, however, a welcome boost to its income.

By 1996 still as many as 98 were reaching the top, all but eleven of them in the two weeks of May which ended with Bruce Herrod's death. It was as if a false sense of security, and therefore taking the summit for granted, had contributed to poor decisions being made. Herrod's death seemed such a tragic waste after the lessons so painfully learned in the storm only two weeks before. Ian Woodall received a savaging from the South African press for his leadership of what had become a controversial expedition.

'Here,' I said, passing a steaming mug to the back of the tent. 'Last brew tonight.' I took a last look at the South-west Face of Everest gradually sinking into blue-black shadows and then zipped the door closed.

'It's a joke, isn't it?' Ray said sipping tentatively at the hot tea.

'Everest?' I looked at him. 'Yeah, a bloody circus.'

'It's weird the way some people get so obsessed. Why not go climbing and walking for the fun of it? You wonder how many fantastic walks and climbs they have passed by and ignored while ticking big names on a spurious list.'

'Yes, it's exactly that these days,' I mumbled. 'An obsession with lists – doing all 277 of the Munroes, the 4000-metre peaks in the Alps, the 8000-metre peaks and the Seven Summits. It's all ego-massaging rubbish.'

'Half the time enjoying the climb has nothing to do with it,' Ray added.

'You know, I reckon Dick Bass has a lot to answer for.'

'It wasn't what he planned though.'

'No, but it was a turning point, wasn't it?' I said. 'After he had been guided up Everest and then went on to do all seven highest continental peaks, he had accidentally created a monster, hadn't he? Everyone read his book and those with plenty of money and time suddenly realised that anyone could climb Everest if you threw enough money at it. He was the one who got this circus of commercial trips going. He made people realise it was possible and unwittingly opened Pandora's box.'

'And a fat lot of good it did for Bruce,' Ray said in a muffled voice as he snuggled down into his sleeping bag.

'It's a shame, isn't it?' I said. 'To think he might have been going slowly because he wanted to take a lot of really good photos.'

'Yeah, and we'll never get to see them, nor him. It makes me wonder what we're doing here.'

'Enjoying ourselves, I hope,' I said brightly.

11

Running on Empty

The morning sun had grown warm enough to start softening the frozen *penitentes* that I had climbed the previous evening. Reaching the sling over the rock spike, I clipped myself in and leaned out over the drop to shout down to Ray that all was clear for him to follow. I looked down at the long lake in the shadows far below, pinched in two at a narrow neck of moraines. The tents of our base camp remained hidden in darkness. Everest, Lhotse and Nuptse were still shrouded in icy shadows, although a corona of sunbeams was beginning to shine above the South Col directly in front of me, a great half-circle of golden spokes spraying up into the morning sky, scintillating bursts of light shooting into the air above the vast shadowed bulk of Everest's mountainous cirque.

I took a deep breath and then exhaled a frosty plume of vapour. The dawn bursting out like some crazed laser light show was uplifting, exhilarating to watch. Another brilliant day, good omens, perfect climbing conditions, weather to die for, it was worth all the hassle just to be there for that one morning on the mountain.

I looked up again as Everest flooded into brilliant life and thought of what Guy Cotter, the director of Adventure Consultants, the trekking and climbing company set up by his friends Rob Hall and Gary Ball, had said to me only a few weeks before when I met him in Kathmandu. We were discussing the various merits of commercial expeditions, particularly to Everest. Guy had been guiding on Pumori when the disastrous storm had trapped Rob high on Everest's summit ridge the previous spring. His traumatic role was to try to persuade his friend by radio to make a last ditch attempt to descend.

Guy had a balanced and open attitude to the mountains. Although he understood my views on Alpine-style climbing, he had calmly pointed out that mine was the approach of a climber who had been brought up in the strong cultural legacy of the European Alpine countries, and that it was not necessarily the cultural view of countries such as Japan, India or Korea. We had no right, he argued with quiet assurance, to impose our cultural and moral values on others. In this he was undoubtedly right but in my book that was no reason why we should do nothing for fear of causing offence. Educating the international climbing community was surely the path to take. After all, being environmentally unsound might be the cultural tradition of one nation but that doesn't mean others should not try to persuade that nation to change its ways in the interests of all.

He did say something, however, that I found impossible to deny. He spoke of his own ascent of Everest on a fine spring morning, guiding clients on the upper reaches of the South-east Ridge, breathing bottled oxygen and clipping to fixed ropes, as a wonderful experience, looking out in the bright sunshine of a perfect day over the world of mountains spread out far below. He acknowledged that to climb without oxygen or fixed ropes would certainly be a purer style of ascent, but nevertheless that day had been a very special, exhilarating moment in his climbing career. When he asked me whether I would not feel the same, I was momentarily speechless. I had to admit that, yes, it would be an experience I would find hard to resist.

I watched as the sun burst in a spray of effervescent gold fringing the snowy crest of the South-east Ridge and imagined what it would feel like to be up there now. Wonderful, I thought with a guilty twinge. I would find it very hard to refuse if someone were to say I was welcome to a free trip with the best commercial outfit climbing the mountain.

That didn't make me a hypocrite. It would never happen, I told myself, so why torture yourself with temptations? Yet I still felt uncomfortable with the thought that I might say yes.

Well, there were any number of things I might say yes to, however wrong they might be, I thought. I am as vulnerable as anyone, and no saint, that's for sure. Being honest with myself was a little disturbing. I heard a distant shout and looked down the ice slope.

I watched the rope twitch as Ray came up the *penitentes* snow slope, climbing quickly and only occasionally grabbing the lead rope that hung from the spike. I belayed him on the second lead rope and grinned as he looked up, and lifted a raised thumb.

'Brilliant,' he said, panting hard as he clipped to the sling. 'If it stays like this, you're right, we'll do it. We are going to bloody do it.'

I clapped him on the shoulder. 'Another couple of pitches and we will be at the Star Buttress.'

Hastily tying in to the lead rope which I had fixed the previous evening, I set off towards a prominent rock face that was guarded on its left side by a crenellated cocks-comb rock ridge topped with a steep hanging meringue of snow ice. As I drew near the rocks I noticed a small pedestal standing proud of the ridge. It looked as if it offered a way of traversing round the spiky ridge and reaching the small hanging star-shaped snowfield after which the rock buttress above had been named.

'Watch me,' I yelled across my shoulder at Ray who was paying close attention to the ropes. 'It's just this one move.'

I fiddled a small wire into a narrow crack and, once confident that it was good, clipped the red rope into it and reached up to jam my hand into the widening crack above. A quick pull up and then an awkward high step with my cramponed right boot saw me teetering on the flat-topped edge of the pedestal. Hanging from their wrist loops, my axes clattered with hollow steel clinks against the rock until I flipped one axe handle into the palm of my hand and stretched up high. A bulge of snow, protruding from the cocks-comb ridge, was threatening to push me over backwards. There was a satisfyingly solid sound as the pick buried itself into firm névé. A hard pull enabled me to complete the manoeuvre and stand upright on top of the pedestal. The bulge of névé pressed against my chest, forcing my back to arch, momentarily pushing me off balance, until a swift blow with the ice hammer, a high kick of my front points into the crest of the ice bulge brought me triumphantly to the bottom of the star snowfield.

I let out a howl of delight. Twenty feet further on, the rope tugged at my harness, and I heard the faint cry of warning from below. A sling over a spike and a well-seated wire and a bomb-proof Friend slotted deeply into an adjacent crack formed a solid anchor. I hung back on the slings and yelled round the corner of the cocks-comb that I was safe and ready to bring Ray up. A muffled reply was swept away on the wind which had sprung up.

After an hour's steady climbing we had traversed up towards the hanging bowl of the icefield and, keeping to its upper edge, had reached the far right-hand side of the rock buttress by mid-afternoon. It was little more than a rope's length in height, and I could see where a mushroom of snow-ice protruded out over the top edge. A deep rocky gash bordered the furthest edge of the buttress, and to the left of that the rock swept up in a smooth wall of grey granite. At close quarters, it looked a much harder proposition than the buttress we had climbed above the camp. It was far less broken, with few ledges and crack systems. However, in a fit of confidence created by the superb conditions and fine sunny weather, I felt sure I could climb it after a short and brutal struggle.

Two hours later, I was still perched forty metres above a shivering Ray in a precarious position that I felt forced to maintain. The climbing had progressed smoothly until a blank sweep of granite slab suddenly stopped me in my tracks. With a heavy rucksack, and wearing big double boots, there was no way I was going to attempt such delicate slab-climbing. As I looked down towards Ray I realised with a sinking feeling that my last piece of protection was ten metres below me and off to my left. If I slipped, I would take a twenty-metre swinging fall in the direction of a sharp-edged pillar on the buttress. I had no intention of breaking my bones doing that. Yet I had to make some kind of move if I was to climb the remaining ten metres of rock.

I spent a long time trying to fiddle a small wire into a thin crack, eventually getting it to bed halfway into the slot. I didn't think it would hold me if I fell on to the wire but it seemed sufficiently strong to take the sideways strain of a tensioned traverse to my right. I leaned tentatively out to the side, keeping my eyes fixed on the wire for the slightest sign of movement. As the rope tightened I shouted for Ray to ease out the slack rope little by little. The metal chock attached to the wire ground into the crack with a nerve-wracking grating noise as my weight came to bear on it. I found myself holding my breath and trying not to think of the great swinging fall if it popped out. It settled into stillness as the rough granite bit into the metal wedge.

Gradually I descended to the right into the rocky gash that I had seen earlier and foolishly dismissed as a possible route. Once I managed to reach the crack running up the back of the groove, I hammered a small Kingpin piton hard into the granite and hastily clipped myself to it with a sigh of relief. Shouted communication with Ray was now all but impossible since I was around the corner, buried in a chimney-crack system, and the wind whipped sounds emanating from it into the ether.

I climbed easily to within five metres of the top of the corner and was stopped once more where the crack petered out and the corner opened into a smooth slab of near vertical ice-worn granite. A large roof of dripping grey rock blackened the sky, and above it I caught a glimpse of the icy bulge of névé from which the melt water was dripping. I stared down at the drop to the distant snowfield. My last runner was in the back of the corner twenty feet beneath me and off to the right. There was the slightest ripple on the surface of the granite slab at knee level, and carefully I rested the edge of my boot against the rough surface before pressing down slowly and with my full weight on the tiny ripple. Suddenly my boot edge slipped and I almost lost balance. I searched for some positive hand-holds that would enable me to make a firm pull upwards, but could find nothing but tiny irregular bumps on the granite slab. At nearly six thousand metres, lumbered with as much mountaineering hardware as I could carry, it was proving impossible to make the delicate friction moves that would get me safely up.

A muted call floated on the wind. I knew that I had spent too long on the pitch and should have abandoned the attempt long ago, but pride and pig-headed obduracy had prevented me from retreating. I made a last tentative step up on to the ripple and found that the boot was holding. I stretched above me with my right hand, spread fingers searching in frantic crab-like motions for the merest edge to grip. I became keenly aware that a slip would hurl me into a swinging arc across the face of the buttress and crashing into the far wall of the corner with sickening force. Rigid mountaineering boots are heavily made for warmth and stiffness not for delicate slab climbing. There would be no warning if the rubber edged soles began creeping off the hold; I would be instantly airborne. A growing sense of insecurity and fear filled my mind, insisting that I back off immediately. It was beyond me.

Once again I was forced to retreat down the buttress, ashamed to admit that the climbing was too hard for me with all the equipment I was carrying. It was a sensible decision, and yet it rankled to have wasted so much time getting nowhere. I was embarrassed to have been rebutted by a short, seemingly innocuous wall. I know that if I had removed my rucksack and really committed myself to a few delicate thin slab moves, I might just have been able to reach the top of the buttress, but I was also keenly aware that the pitch was poorly protected, and the consequences of a fall didn't bare thinking about. As a two-man team, self-rescue wasn't an option I wanted to have to consider again.

'What the hell have you been doing?' Ray demanded when at last I reached his stance. 'I couldn't see anything or hear what you were saying.'

'Look, I'm sorry, but it was really thin.' At once I regretted not having another go at the wall. 'The gear was frightening,' I added sheepishly.

'Well, I'm frozen,' Ray said sharply. I glanced at my watch and was horrified to see how much time I had wasted. 'I've been in shadow down here for the last hour and the wind is a killer.' Ray shivered and stamped his feet.

'I'm sorry, I can't climb this, so we'll have to go round. Unless you want a go.'

'Okay, but let's get on with it. Which way, left or right?'

'Right, I reckon.' I leaned around the pedestal to which Ray had belayed and looked down into a broken couloir of shattered rocks and dirty grey ice. It was pitted with rocks impacted into its surface. Two hundred feet below us a spray of black dust on the snow at the bottom of the couloir showed where recent rock falls had scoured the ice. 'We'll have to move quickly, mind.'

'Christ! It looks lethal,' Ray exclaimed as he leaned over my shoulder. 'I'm not going in there.'

'It's not that bad . . .'

'It bloody well is. Look at that lot.' He was pointing to where the couloir reared up to form a vertical chimney blocked with huge, precariously-balanced piles of heavy rocks. On either side shattered rocks were stacked like shelves of heavy grey quarry tiles. 'If that goes, we won't stand a chance . . .'

'Okay,' I interrupted, 'that's why we have to be quick, and we can only make it at that one spot.' I pointed to the narrow bed of the gully that we would have to cross during a diagonal abseil down from the pedestal. 'If you climb that short corner there, you'll be safe in seconds. Once you get round that point, nothing can hit you.'

'I'm not going in there in a month of Sundays,' Ray snapped. I peered into the couloir again, wondering whether I was wrong. I could see all the possible dangers, and the couloir certainly had a menacing atmosphere to it, but it still seemed feasible to cross it. Ray looked angry. Cold and the long wait had made him justifiably irritable.

'It's a risk, I know, but an acceptable one.' Ray shook his head at me, so I continued: 'Nothing has come down it so far today, has it? Have you heard anything falling in all the time you've stood here?'

'Well, no, but that doesn't . . .'

'Sure it doesn't,' I cut him off. 'But look at our options. We can't go up or pass it on the left, so we either make the abseil, or that's it, we go down, the route is over.'

There was a long silence as Ray contemplated the couloir.

'Sod it,' he swore testily. 'Give me the bloody rope then. I'll do it.'

He quickly set up a system by which I could abseil him down the couloir and at the same time belay him when he crossed to the other side.

'You'll have to untie the red, thread the piton and use it as a back rope when you come down,' he said as he leaned out from the pedestal and prepared to descend. 'Untie and pull it through when you get to the other side. Right, let's go, and do it slow,' he cautioned as I released the rope and he stepped gingerly down into the shattered walls of the couloir.

I felt suddenly very frightened for him. It was obvious that he thought he had been cornered into making the abseil. I was happy to do it, and thought the risk an acceptable one, but had I any right to impose it on Ray? I watched as he edged across a small ledge that traversed the very steep rocky bed of the couloir. I could see that the tottering heap of loose rock was now directly above him. A sudden clatter of falling rocks made me glance quickly down at Ray. He was steadying himself, gripping a sharp hand-hold and watching the ledge on which he had been standing tumble down towards the blackened ice far below.

'Slack!' he yelled. I could hear the nervous edge to his voice.

I let out some more rope and he scurried across the bed of the couloir, where a stream of meltwater poured down, and reached the corner I had pointed out to him. There he stopped to examine the way ahead, unsure of how best to continue. Glancing up at the menacing rock chimney, I silently urged him to hurry, though I could understand his caution because he was no longer abseiling but actually trying to climb up and diagonally away from me. A fall would result in a punishing swing down into the broken bed of the couloir. That fall would almost certainly trigger a dangerous amount of rock fall as the rope scythed across the mess of perched blocks. He stepped tentatively into the corner and reached to grasp the flat ledge at the top. He struggled for a moment to swing on to the ledge, his cramponed feet kicking in the air as he fought to convert the awkward mantleshelf move into a balanced standing position.

At last, almost in slow motion, he managed to rock forward on to the ledge and stand up. He waved up to me with a broad grin and then began to arrange a secure anchor for my crossing. Where he stood, the ledge was sheltered from the couloir by a protective roof above him and slightly to one side. I could see a possible line leading up behind him towards a steep snow-slope.

'What's it like?' I yelled impatiently, and the sound of my voice echoed around the walls of the couloir. I flinched, half expecting to hear the clatter and whip crack sounds of rock fall.

'Okay,' Ray called, raising his thumb. 'Just be quick.'

I nodded and looked nervously at the dark chimney. The wind tugged at my back and I was suddenly aware of how cold I had become while waiting that short time for Ray to make the crossing. The buttress was completely in shadow now that it was late afternoon and the cold November temperature suddenly made itself keenly felt. Carefully I arranged the back rope and, protected by Ray's control on it, descended reluctantly into the couloir. It was now easy to appreciate why Ray had been so concerned. As soon as I was committed to the descent, the couloir became a claus-trophobic place with a frightening, intimidating ambience. The whole place was still, as if waiting for something to happen. I teetered across the ledge, which had been partially demolished by Ray, and winced as I kicked some loose rocks into the couloir below. I watched them gain speed and career away from me, as if mesmerised by their progress. I stared at the explosive bursts of dust where they impacted and then ricocheted off the walls. The air filled with that distinctive smell of scorched and shattered stone. It was a fearful scent, reminiscent of the terror and helplessness that big rock falls can induce. The atmosphere created a crushing sensation, as if the potential avalanche of tons of rock from the chimney above was already pressing down on me. I hurried towards the distant security of the corner, almost holding my breath as I climbed.

Suddenly I was pulled to a halt from behind just as I was in the very centre of the couloir. While the blue lead rope with which Ray was belaying me tugged me forward at my waist, the red rope was pulling me backwards. *Damn it! The back rope!* I had forgotten about it, and now, at the most exposed point, it was preventing me from going forward or back.

'Slack,' I yelled up to Ray who was out of sight safely ensconced on his ledge. 'The bloody back rope's jammed.' I heard the same nervous shake in my voice that Ray's had betrayed. I fumbled with the red knot at my waist, trying to untie the bowline knot as quickly as possible. A sudden crashing report made me duck down and then look anxiously around. My heart seemed to be trying to hammer its way out of my chest. A fist-size stone spat down the couloir in a vicious spinning flight with dust bursting as if hit by machine gun fire as it clattered off the walls.

I cowered against the rock wall of the couloir, hunching my head into my neck, trying to make my entire body smaller than the kevlar helmet on my head. There was a creaking noise from somewhere in the couloir. I darted my head from side to side, trying to guess the direction of the next fusillade.

'Shit, shit . . . ' I was swearing as I pulled the knot clear and began to haul the rope down from where it was threaded through the piton at the abseil station far above me. At first it refused to move. My heart sank at the thought of having to climb back up the wall of shattered rocks. Then the rope began to creep forward, and I heaved down hard, forcing it through the tight constriction of the eye of the piton as fast as I could.

'Tight!' I yelled, and the blue rope tugged reassuringly at my waist.

'Watch out for the back rope,' I heard Ray yell. 'It may start a rock fall.'

'I'm bloody well aware of that,' I muttered under my breath. I gave a last tug and the red rope soared into the air above me and hurtled down in twisting coils. Before it had hit the first rocks I was scrambling up the corner as fast as I could. Dislodged rocks began to tumble into the depths below as I lay on my belly on the edge of the ledge, grunting, panting and wriggling furiously as Ray laughed.

'What's so funny?' I snapped when I got to my feet.

'Your face,' Ray said.

'Can you see into the narrows?' I nodded towards the distant ice slope, unable to say any more for want of breath.

'Yeah, I think so,' Ray said. 'I had a look round the corner, and you were right, this leads round into the base of the narrows.'

I felt suddenly confident again. For a moment we seemed to have been derailed, but now it looked as if we could reach the top of the buttress by a narrow ice couloir that we had spotted during our binocular reconnaissance at base camp. It swept up through a rocky defile on the right side of the buttress. At first we had dismissed it, worried as we were that it was also a perfect funnel for anything falling from above. All along we had also been anxious about the dangerous avalanche conditions on the entire mountain, and so we had decided that these narrows were too risky.

'Told you so.' I grinned as Ray took a playful swipe at me. 'That wasn't so bad, was it? And now that it's been in shadow for a while the snow should be pretty well frozen,' I added.

Two hours later, as darkness began to wash over the frozen shadowed face, I watched while Ray tackled a steep chute of ice to the right of an awkward rock step at the top of the narrows. Gusts of wind tugged at my jacket and I shivered convulsively. I was annoyed with myself for wasting so much time on the buttress which had now left us climbing in the early evening with night soon upon us and still with nowhere to pitch the tent. We should have been snug in our sleeping bags, drinking hot tea and soup instead of getting uncomfortably cold and tired in the confined icy gloom of the narrows. A spray of snow whipped across my face. I looked up at the darkening sky surprised to see that clouds had swept in, unseen by us, from the other side of the mountain. I began to worry about the weather as the wind increased and snow began to fall. Had it broken? How exposed were we to avalanches on this new line we had chosen?

There was a distant muffled cry from above and three distinct tugs at my waist signalling me to climb up. I stripped the belay quickly, hammering out the two wires from a frozen crack with the pick of my axe and then unwinding the ice screw as fast as my shaking hands would allow. Ten minutes of brisk climbing up steep water ice soon warmed me up. As I pulled over the bulge at the top of the narrows I could just see the shadowy hunched figure of Ray on a snow arête high above me to the right. I caught the flash of his head torch momentarily before it disappeared in a flurry of snow.

'What do you reckon?' I called as I clipped into his belay. 'Seen anywhere to bivi?' A muffled reply drifted down through the gusting snowflakes. 'I thought I saw a rock outcrop which might be okay, over on the left.'

'Right,' I said, grabbing the ice screws from his waist. 'No point hanging around here. See you in a bit.'

I reached up, turned on my torch and then stepped on to the steep and snow ice. With the wind strengthening, the face had become a hostile unwelcoming place. Somewhere above us in the gloom a double band of seracs stood like serried ranks of fangs. As far as we had been able to tell through binoculars, these appeared to be old seracs that had crumbled, though they seemed stable enough. With seracs, you can never be sure.

The rope came tight at my waist just as I spotted a dark mass in the gloom above me. Snow danced in the yellow light from my torch, reflecting like fire flies in car headlights. I killed the light and looked again. Yes, there it was, just as Ray had said. It was still far out of my reach, perhaps a rope's length away.

Ray soon joined me and headed at once for the rocky shadows. A muffled yell came down through the snowfall surprisingly quickly; my optimism had been rewarded. I hurried up the slope, climbing with urgent speed, hoping against hope that there would be a perfect tent site, with rock belays and protection from anything falling from above.

'It's not brilliant,' Ray said as I surveyed the site. Far from being a steep buttress providing shelter from rock fall or avalanches, it was only a smooth slab of granite set into the slope like a beached whale. We peered hopefully from side to side, head torch beams criss-crossing through the snowflakes.

'There's a good crack here, and over there, for pitons,' Ray said without much enthusiasm.

'Yeah, but *look* at it!' I said, pointing at the slabby rocks. 'Anything coming down will sweep over this like a tidal wave. We wouldn't stand a chance . . . '

'Well, we don't have much of a choice,' Ray snapped a little testily. We were both cold and tired and the tension was making us irritable. I turned away, ignoring him, while I tried to decide whether it was better to camp here or keep going in the dark. I switched off my torch and glanced around. The wind seemed to have dropped a little and there was less snow blasting against my face. I looked at the sky. There were some clear patches in the cloud cover above, a few stars sparkling in the dark gaps. For a moment it seemed a little lighter, and I glanced up at the face above.

'There,' I said suddenly, pointing urgently. Ray followed my finger.

'A serac?' he said incredulously. 'You want to camp under a serac?'

'Well, yes, if it's stable.' I stared fixedly at the distant, barely distinguishable, grey-white shadowy tooth on the face above. 'It's not so far away. I might as well have a look. We've got to go that way in the morning.'

'I suppose so,' Ray muttered.

'Look,' I reasoned, 'if it's no good, I'll abseil straight back down and we can dig a platform here. Okay?'

'Go on then.'

I grabbed the gear from Ray's harness, looped some long slings around my neck and set off.

'Just be quick about it. I'm bloody perished,' he yelled as I kicked up the frozen slope above.

At the farthest stretch of the rope I could just reach the ice wall of the serac. From what I could see in the limited visibility, it was a stable structure of icicle-fringed water ice. It protruded from the face like a sinking ship's prow breaching the surface of the sea. Its angled deck formed the gently overhanging face of ice under which we could hack out a tent platform. The tent could be safely secured with ice screws buried deep in the hard water ice of the serac. I tied off the red rope and yelled down into the night for Ray to use it as a handrail as he came up. Meanwhile I set about preparing the platform.

Two hours of exhausting work, hacking at hard blue ice in the dark, had cleared a small platform for the tent. It was a bit too narrow, and so the sides overhung the ledge, but it was firmly lashed down to five ice screws and wasn't going anywhere.

'What about the seracs above this one?' Ray asked as we struggled to squeeze into the tiny blue shelter. I handed in my rucksacks for him to store away in the rear tube.

'I think they're all fairly stable,' I said, nervously checking the ice screws for the umpteenth time.

'Yeah, you're right.' Ray smiled. 'I just never feel comfortable being around these buggers, however solid they seem.'

'Don't worry about the whole thing falling down,' I said, glancing up at the icicles hanging out into space from the lip of the serac wall forty feet above the tent. 'If one of those broke off it would go straight through the tent like a javelin.'

Ray dismissed the idea. 'Naw. I looked at them earlier. They'll fall too far out to hit us, but if a big serac went I was wondering . . .'

'I tell you, we're in by far the safest place.' I lit the gas stove which burst into roaring blue light. 'If we had stopped by those slabs, we would have been hit by everything. At least here it would take a really huge one to threaten us, and even then I reckon we would be okay.'

There was a spluttering noise from the stove and the blue flame faltered, roared back to full power, and then went out completely. I grabbed the stove and shook it vigorously. I checked to see whether water or snow had got on to the burner. It was quite dry, and despite my efforts, it wouldn't relight.

'Oh shit!' I muttered to myself.

'What's wrong?'

'Stove's buggered.' I unscrewed the cylinder and shook it in the tent. I could clearly feel the sloshing liquid weight of the gas. 'Damn. It's still half full.'

'Well try another cylinder. You never know.'

The stove with the new cylinder burst into light at the flick of my gas lighter and we both breathed a sigh of relief. I searched through the plastic bag of gas cylinders and found the one I had changed the previous evening, which I had marked with a distinctive scratch. I shook it to confirm it too was half full. I threw both half empty cylinders on to Ray's sleeping bag.

'We're in trouble, mate,' I said as I watched him shake the cylinders. 'For some reason we're only able to burn half the contents. The rest is still in there, or something is . . .'

'You don't think . . .'

'Yes,' I said bitterly. 'I can't think of anything else. Damn it.' I pounded my fist against the coiled rope pillow. I suspected that we had been sold dodgy gas in Kathmandu. We had heard of the practice of some unscrupulous dealers of injecting half empty cylinders with water so that they were restored to their full weight as printed on the side. There was no way of telling. The propane butane mix would still come out of the cartridge and burn effectively enough until we were left with a canister half full of water.

'Oh Jesus,' Ray groaned. 'How much have we got left then?'

'Three and this one I've just fitted,' I replied. 'We planned four bivis and reckoned on using one canister per day between the two of us, so I stuffed in an extra can just to be on the safe side. I hate going short on gas, *hate* it.'

'Well, how much more do we need?' I watched as Ray counted the nights off on his fingers. 'We've made far better progress than we thought. I mean, we had planned this camp to be way down by the star buttress, so . . .'

'At least two more camps, possibly three if there's no gas at Camp I on the normal route,' I interrupted.

'We're okay then,' Ray said with a grin. 'You said we've got four left.'

'You're forgetting that they are four half cans, i.e. two.'

'Ah . . . We'll just have to ration the hot food then,' Ray suggested, 'but keep the fluid quantities up. Remember, too, that these conditions are far better than we reckoned, so we should do it quicker.'

'There are a lot of ifs in all this,' I said doubtfully, 'but I suppose it is possible if we manage to reach the summit ridge tomorrow night, top out next day and get down to Camp I the day after that. If we reach their fixed ropes we might be able to descend all the way to their advanced base camp and get gas there,' I mused.

'Not a bad idea these fixed ropes, are they?' Ray looked at me and grinned. We both laughed at our hypocrisy.

'Yeah, well,' I said at last. 'We wouldn't need them if it wasn't for this dodgy gas. We'd still have gone up in the best possible style.'

'What about the polypropylene we fixed in the bottom couloir?'

'That was just to get a fast springboard on to the face, and we didn't really need them.'

'Still put them in,' Ray admonished. 'You're right, we didn't need them, and I wish we hadn't now. They'll be more trouble than help in the end.'

The next morning we slept late and then made a lazy start after the late night. A strong wind kept blasting clouds of spindrift in hissing surges against the tent fabric. Brewing inside the tent was the only option, and I hung the stove by its chains from the topmost point of the tent. The gas purred away reassuringly and condensation soon formed on the aluminium pots stacked full of snow and ice chippings. As my head was nearest the door I was unaware of any ventilation problems. Indeed the slightly open door flap was a nuisance as it allowed gusts of powder snow to spray across my sleeping bag. I was forced to keep brushing it off. Ray lay with his head at the far end, partly jammed against the long rear storage tube. The rucksacks stuffed down the tube prevented any ventilation from entering via the mesh entrance at that end.

When I passed the final steaming mug of tea to Ray he seemed subdued. At first I dismissed it as tiredness and set about getting organised for the day. I glanced out of the door as I sipped the last of my tea and watched the sun shining across the South Col. It really was a quite stunning place to be. We had seen this view every morning for weeks and were no longer amazed. It always astonished me how easy it was to take wonderful things for granted so quickly. A great plume of snow and ice was stretching away from Everest's summit, a sure sign that the jet stream winds were tearing into the upper flanks of the mountain. Soon, as winter advanced and the winds tore into the mountain at more than a hundred miles per hour, the white coating of monsoon snow would be stripped away and the South-west Face would become an bleak black pyramid.

'Wind's easing up a bit,' I said and ducked my head back into the tent. 'Sun will be here in a minute. Looks like another fine day in paradise.' There was no reply from Ray. 'If the snow stays good, and the seracs are like this one, we should reach the gully leading through the rock band to the summit ridge before dark.' I felt a thrill of excitement course through me, delighted to be on the mountain at last and getting to grips with the climbing. 'Should be grand.'

'I'm not sure,' Ray said in a quiet voice from the back of the tent. I glanced over to see him lying on his side, propped up on one elbow and covering his eyes with his other hand.

'What's wrong?' I asked with a sinking feeling.

'Feel dreadful,' came the chilling reply.

'How do you mean, dreadful?' I asked anxiously. 'Did you not sleep?'

'Yes, yes, I slept fine.' Ray looked up and met my gaze. 'I was okay when I woke, but now I feel awful.'

'Is it your breathing? Or nausea? Do you feel sick? Or . . .'

'It's my head,' Ray said slowly. 'I've got this dreadful headache. It's getting worse. I thought the tea would help it go away, but it has got worse.'

I stared helplessly at my friend, wishing he were okay, hoping it was nothing serious. I was surprised at myself, at how quickly I came to the decision.

'Right, let's get out of here,'

'What?' Ray looked up in surprise.

'We're going down, now, while we can.'

'I'm sorry, Joe. It's just . . .' He trailed off, refusing to look at me.

'There's nothing to be sorry about, mate,' I said, not looking at him. I was scared for him and didn't want him to know it. 'Come on, let's get our shit together and get out of here.' I shuffled the sleeping bag off my legs and began to change into my climbing clothes.

There really never was a choice. A part of me felt absolutely crushed that the climb was over; that just when everything had seemed so good we should have to retreat. If Ray had what I suspected he might have, we had to get down fast. In 1990, on Ama Dablam, he had suffered a minor stroke while walking up to Camp I. We didn't know it at the time. He just seemed to become instantly unacclimatised and kept falling over. He was muttering incoherently, talking all sorts of gobble-de-gook, as if suffering from aphasia. He kept saying things like, 'You go down to the summit whilst I go up to Camp five' when there were only two camps on the mountain. It was all very confusing, as well as being dangerously funny, so that we couldn't take him seriously. He managed to stagger back down to base camp and next morning, feeling completely recovered, he came back up to find me waiting for him. Over the next four days we climbed the mountain un-aware that a small blood clot had broken away and caused his potentially deadly symptoms. When he returned home, he consulted Tat, who said that, had he been on the trip, he wouldn't have let Ray out of base camp with the symptoms since it was almost certainly a stroke. A brain scan revealed no damage or residual problems. I joked that, for a man with a single cell amoeba for a brain, it wasn't so surprising. Now it seemed as if the joke had back-fired on me.

Once again, he was suffering from head problems and my immediate thought was of Ama Dablam six years before. Was it more likely to happen again because of that one incident? There was no logical reason for him to be any more sus-ceptible than I to another stroke, but there was no way I was going to take the risk. Ray muttered an apologetic agreement to my plan and began to get ready. He moved slowly with his head bowed. I could sense that he felt terrible for letting me down just when everything had seemed to be going so well. I wanted to put an arm round him, and give him a hug, and tell him it meant nothing and not to worry. I turned away, unable to make that small gesture. I grabbed my harness and buckled it round my waist, feeling angry at my mute reticence.

Just as I was stuffing my sleeping bag into my rucksack with the food, stove and gas canisters I felt a vibration gradually building. I looked up and caught Ray's eye. We stared at one another as the vibration became a thunderous sound that we recognised with chilling certainty. The seracs had gone! I was unable to speak, paralysed by the roar of the approaching avalanche. How big was it? Were we safe? Oh Christ! Don't let it hit us! I could almost see Ray's thoughts mirror mine in his wide-eyed stare. Was this the end? Pieces of ice falling from our serac struck the goretex walls of the tent as the ground shook. The noise built up into a roar. I held my breath and stared fixedly at the tent walls, waiting for them to implode. Suddenly, with the sound of an express train roaring inches past the tent, a monstrous plume of ice and snow went ripping past our campsite. I broke from our locked stare and stuck my head out of the tent. Less than twenty metres away a huge avalanche was rushing at ferocious speed down the couloir to our right. There were momentary glimpses of ice blocks as hundreds of tons of debris hurtled towards the glacier thousands of feet below. Then there was silence, broken by two long exhalations from two deeply frightened men. Through the open door a spray of ice crystals swished softly on to the sleeping bag I was crushing into my fists. We looked at each other lost for words. Then Ray leaned forward, reached an arm around my shoulder and gave me a big hug.

'Good tent site,' he said, and we threw back our heads and roared with laughter.

'We were dead,' I said at last. 'I really thought we were dead.' Ray stopped laughing and nodded.

'Come on, let's get down quickly.'

By early evening we were staggering under huge loads along the moraines banks of the lake near base camp. In the distance we could see the tents, and approaching quickly were Tony Halliwell, Richard Haszko, Bruce French and Pertemba, coming to welcome us back and help us with the loads. It had been a long descent, complicated by a very crevassed couloir which we had abseiled directly to avoid the traverse back across the dangerous rock couloir next to the star buttress. Ray seemed to have recovered by the time we reached the glacier, but we both knew there was no going back up the mountain. For us, the expedition, the new route, was over.

Tony, Ric, and Steve would soon make their attempt on the normal route, and Steve would eventually succeed in reaching the summit, but for Ray and me, it was over.

Two days later, as they set off to make their summit bid, Ray and I packed our gear into our barrels and, leaving them in the cook tent, set off on the beautiful trek over the Tsho La via the Gokyo valley and back to Namche Bazar. I turned once at the moraines above Gorak Shep and looked at the beautiful pyramid of Pumori that had cost us so much in time and effort and wondered if it had been worth it. All that hassle just for a couple of days' freedom on the hill? I looked at Everest, Nuptse and Lhotse, quiet and unspoilt at this late date in the season, with no climbers inhabiting the base camp. In a little over four months the huge numbers would be back, building their tented city, nailing the mountain down with their ropes like Lilliputians swarming over Gulliver. It was an awesome and beautiful sight – serene, enchanted it seemed, in that calm frozen morning air, pristine and inviolate for the moment.

12

The Numbers Game

As Ray walked towards the crest of a grassy spur that ran down from the hillside above Lobuche, directly ahead of him loomed the north face of Cholatse, falling precipitously into a dark and shadowed lake at its foot. I swung my rucksack from my shoulders and bent down to retrieve my water bottle. I stared at the mountain while I quenched my thirst, remembering how Mal Duff and I had found an intimidating line to climb and had teased one another about giving it a try. I recognised several of the features that we had identified five years before. The line was still there, unclimbed, a project waiting to happen. I thought of rushing to catch up with Ray and asking whether he would be interested in coming back here for a go at the face. Then I remembered how disappointed he was with our attempt on Pumori. I turned my back on Cholatse and sat down on my rucksack.

The sun was pleasantly warm on my face and the sky gin clear with approaching winter's clarity. I could see for miles. A breathtaking horizon of icy peaks stretched before me. I looked towards Everest, towering above everything, with an icy plume trailing away from the summit. I felt confused. A welter of conflicting emotions made me feel outraged and hypocritical, sad and angry, all at once. I knew that if the opportunity to climb Everest suddenly came my way, I would find it hard to resist, and yet I felt angry that some people should have behaved so badly on the world's highest mountain and allowed it to get into such a mess.

There is nothing inherently wrong or sinister about those climbing on the mountain. Whatever their motivations might be, I feel sure that most of the guides and their clients are as appalled as I am by some of the events that have taken place in recent years. If so many people want to climb the mountain, then inevitably there will be a heavy impact on its environment. There is no point harking back to some nostalgic notion of a golden age in the past – as if we could ever return to that time. Perhaps it is inevitable that it should have come to this state of affairs. There are simply too many people wanting to be here for it not to have happened. Air travel has shrunk the world and the values and mores of that society from which the early climbers came have long since gone. An ascent of Everest can never be what it was two decades or more ago. It too has been shrunk.

If a few have behaved badly, then perhaps their actions will have so disgusted their fellow climbers that there will be urgent pressure for it never to happen again. Climbing Everest, or any of the eight-thousand-metre peaks, is after all only a small part of mountaineering as a whole. If the significance of such ascents is put into a proper perspective, then perhaps the pressure to succeed at any cost may diminish. It seems strange at a time when the technical standards of mountaineering have reached such extraordinary heights that just collecting high altitude summits by any means available should attract any acknowledgement or prestige.

Or have I got it all wrong? Could the behaviour of those who ignore dying men be no different from the natural way of animals faced with injury or death in the wild?

I stood up, hefted my rucksack on to my shoulders and set off after Ray. We hoped to reach the Green Valley Lodge just before the start of the Tsho La pass which would bring us down into the Gokyo valley the next day. As the hillside darkened with evening shadows and the temperature plummeted I hurried forward, hoping I had remembered to pack my head torch. I turned for one last look at Everest resplendent in a golden sunset. I doubted that I would return. In less than a week I would be back in Sheffield, and for once it seemed that the day could not come sooner.

Within a week of my homecoming I was due in Holland for publication of the Dutch edition of *Storms of Silence*. One evening I found myself in front of an attentive live television audience, being interviewed on a Dutch 'talk show' named after its presenter 'Karel'. When I took my place at the table, Karel, an intelligent and perceptive interviewer, began with some familiar questions about what had happened in Peru in 1985 and then asked me what I thought about the video tape excerpt they were about to show. A monitor lit up in front of me, and there was Ronald Naar, talking to camera in his tent on the South Col while a dying man lay outside, unseen, thirty yards away. It looked very calm in the tent, with no sign of flapping canvas and no sound of shrieking winds outside. The film's soundtrack was in Dutch, but I was given a verbatim translation (so I was assured) of what he said.

'We had slept for three hours,' Naar said to the camera, 'when Materma, our Sherpa, had to go to the toilet. The spindrift had calmed down a little bit. And he suddenly said, "There is somebody outside on the ground and he is waving at us." So I looked outside and saw a down jacket which lifted its hand now and then and waved with it from right to left. It was evident that he had a bad case of hypothermia. He was lying on the path down, so the Indians must have walked past him this morning on their descent. They must have seen him; I don't know what they did or what they decided at that moment. It is not a pleasant sight, seeing him out there. If I look at the zipper of my tent, I can still see that hand lifting before me. Maybe he is still waving, but I don't want to see it any more. The point is, we can't do anything for him. Somebody who is in that state has a body temperature of 26 to 28 degrees Celsius. He is heavy. He has a huge body. We cannot move him. If we give him hot liquid, he will die. These are the things you experience on Everest.'

'But he is dying out there,' the horrified voice of the cameraman says from behind the lens.

'I don't know if you have ever been in a hospital,' Naar responds. 'In intensive care people are dying too. It sounds cruel, but you can't do anything about this. I can sacrifice my own life for him, but that would be pointless.'

I was astounded by that analogy. How could 'intensive care' be compared with the South Col? The film scene changed. The man had since died. The camera shot panned unsteadily across the Col, showing a view of the frozen corpse of the Indian climber while the soundtrack recorded the cameraman in tears, exclaiming: 'This is really hard to do. Shit, man! Look at him.'

The studio audience was ominously quiet as the film ended and Karel asked me what I thought of this behaviour. For a moment I didn't know what to say. I was keenly aware that I was about to criticise someone who, for all I knew, might have been a Dutch sporting hero. I think my expression said it all, and when I turned the question round on Karel and asked what he thought of it – not as a mountaineer, but as a man – I was glad to hear his shocked and angry response. It seemed fairly obvious from the loud applause of the audience that they thought very much the same.

I left the studio in two minds, unsure whether I should have ducked the question. Then I admonished myself for cowardice. I have a very clear view of that sort of behaviour. I knew that my reluctance was due to more than not wanting to be seen criticising people. I didn't want to step on toes, didn't want to make enemies of those who had a vested interest in the status quo. I had no idea how many other people felt as I did, how many knew about the incident and other recent events in the region, and whether they even cared.

Climbers have a rare ability to gamble the rest of their lives on one step, and for this they are both admired and sometimes regarded as vainly stupid. They take to extreme the notion of Deep Play, whereby what they stand to win from their gamble can never equal the enormity of what they will lose. The maxim 'If you want something, you have to take a risk; if you really want something, you have to risk everything,' seems well suited to some of the more dangerous aspects of mountaineering.

Death and high drama have always been synonymous with high altitude climbing. Seven Sherpas died in an avalanche below Everest's North Col on the British 1922 expedition – only the second attempt to be made to scale the world's highest peak. The 1934 German expedition to Nanga Parbat ended in the lingering deaths of nine men, a disaster which, for sheer protracted agony, has no parallel in climbing annals. In the mid-seventies eight Soviet women on Peak Lenin were engulfed in a harrowing storm in which they selflessly attempted to remain together so as to look after each other. Consequently, all eight perished. On K2, in the summer of 1986, thirteen climbers died in a single season. Fatal accidents are a recurrent theme in the history of mountaineering, and there will certainly be many more with the incredible surge in numbers visiting the greater ranges.

Eleven climbers perished on Everest in the spring season of 1996 (twelve if you count the Sherpa who died later in hospital), while 87 reached the summit. When one realises that, historically, for every six ascents someone on the mountain has died (at present 156 deaths to 932 ascents), that traumatic season turns out to have been safer than average. Climbing Everest has always been an extremely dangerous undertaking that in the past has killed many of the world's elite climbers. Whether guided clients of limited experience should be paying to experience such risks is a moot point. That eight people died in a single terrible storm in May was tragic but predictable, given the traffic jams. While there will always be disasters in the mountains, this one could have been avoided. That more did not die in that storm is due to good luck rather than good timing, though the exemplary conduct of many of those caught up in it undoubtedly saved lives. The wasted Indian lives on the north side and the behaviour of the Japanese do not bear comparison. If they had been climbing in small groups, possibly Alpine-style and without oxygen, I am sure they would never have pushed on so late in the day. A total ban on oxygen would reduce the number attempting the peak and help to cut down both the death rate and pollution. A reckless few, unaware of their own limitations, might still try climbing without oxygen and kill themselves. But a ban would significantly reduce the number of marginally competent climbers risking both large sums of money and their lives on a summit attainable 'by fair means' only by the world's elite mountaineers.

Some climbers have risked their lives, others have died, selflessly attempting to rescue fellow mountaineers, regardless of fault or criticism. Others have sat by and zipped the door shut on a man's final lonely end. Some have tried to climb the mountain in the purest style by new routes while the majority seem to care not at all for such fine ethical notions and reduce the mountain's height and seriousness by breathing bottled oxygen and hauling up on fixed ropes. Some say they are cheating, others think it is perfectly acceptable.

Who is to say that one way of getting to the top of a mountain is any better than another? Indeed, who has the right, or for that matter the authority, to make such a judgement? Is it down to the national bodies representing mountaineering in the different countries, or to individuals lobbying for some sort of change? Perhaps some responsibility should be laid at the door of the Nepalese government for allowing its guardianship of one of the world's great symbols to become so devalued.

I suppose my reaction to the worst examples of bad behaviour is an emotional one, devoid of the hard-nosed pragmatism displayed by more ambitious high altitude climbers. I find it unforgivable that climbers can treat their fellow mountaineers with such callous disregard. It has nothing to do with whether or not rescue appears to be possible but everything to do with being humane, caring individuals who can see the passing of a life for what it is, and not simply an inconvenient obstacle to realising egotistic ambitions. If shutting the door on a man's last imploring gesture, or avoiding eye contact while climbing sternly past three dying men, are the requisite skills for modern high altitude climbing, then I want none of it.

It is not enough to say that these incidents are rare and exceptional occurrences. Too many Everest climbers have been prepared to accept the mess on the South Col as a reasonable price to pay. Commercial companies, and those guides who have firsthand knowledge of the state of the mountain, are still prepared to sell and lead trips through a field of tattered tents, oxygen cylinders and abandoned corpses. Karl Huyberechts's shocking photograph, taken on the South Col in the spring of 1989, says so much more than words can. It is a damning indictment of the way in which climbers have abused the mountain and of how far people are prepared to go to reach the summit of Everest. It does not matter if some attempts have since been made to clean up the mess. The fact that we ever let it get into such a deplorable state remains a shameful legacy. When he sent the photograph to me, he told me that the body in the lower left-hand corner was that of the Sherpa, Lakpa Dorje, from Kunde village, near Namche. He had died during a winter expedition in 1988 and, as far as Karl knew, the corpse was still there. Karl himself was last on Everest in 1992, when Ronald Naar was camped on the South Col. In 1994 Karl tried to organise a clean-up expedition with Pierre Royer, but it failed due to a lack of interest.

Since then a successful incentive scheme has been enthusiastically supported by all the guiding companies. Sherpas are paid a cash sum for each empty oxygen bottle brought down from the South Col, as a result of which some 800 bottles have been retrieved from the upper mountain. It has been reported, however, that as many as a thousand still remain up there, littering the site of Camp IV.

I understand why people might want to climb Everest. An ascent of the highest peak will always be a significant social cachet. For the professional climber, its addition to his or her mountaineering *curriculum vitae* will be bound to increase the chances of either sponsorship or employment as a guide. Although diminished in reputation, Everest is still regarded by an ill-informed general public as the ultimate mountaineering achievement. In most countries an ascent of Everest is still held to be an heroic endeavour. Such national acclaim can be a source of considerable wealth and prestige for the opportune climber lucky enough to make a first ascent for his or her country. Few, if any, of these Everest climbers ever make any comment about the state of the mountain or the style of ascents.

How many will have died on the mountain after another twenty years of several hundred climbers attempting Everest each season? How many of those corpses will be removed? Will the area of the South Col and above begin to resemble some grisly charnel house in years to come?

How long will it be before some permanent pressurised huts are constructed on the South Col? It sounds fanciful, but in 1912, as Scott lay dying in the polar wasteland that he described as 'this awful place', it would have been inconceivable to his team, or Amundsen's, that in less than fifty years a community of scientists would be living at the South Pole all year round. On the Tibetan side of Everest an hotel is to be built on or near the site of the old pre-war Rongbuk base camp. I wonder what Mallory or Irvine would have thought of that?

If climbers 'cannot afford morality', and ethical behaviour becomes too expensive, then has the sport become prostituted? Since when did means ever justify the end in mountaineering? I wonder what Shipton or Tilman or Herzog would have thought of this circus today. Would the likes of Shackleton, Whymper or Mummery ever have behaved in this manner? They were all highly ambitious and no less egotistic individuals, but frankly I cannot for one moment see them approving the sort of farce that is presently going on in the Khumbu. Is that solely because they were a product of their time, and the values of that society?

When Tilman reached the summit of Nanda Devi with Noel Odell in 1936, a feat described at the time by Shipton as 'the finest mountaineering achievement ever performed in the Himalayas . . . a brilliant example of a light expedition', no one thought to doubt them. At the time, it was the highest mountain ever climbed, and it had been accomplished virtually in Alpine-style. Now such comparable achievements have to be backed by photographic proof, or else the climbing world will suspect some form of cheating has taken place. There is one cause for this, and that is money. The climbers of Tilman's day stood to gain little other than personal satisfaction and the praise of their peers. Today equivalent feats can ensure you a job for life. Whether Tomo Cesen did or did not solo the South Face of Lhotse and the North Face of Jannu is a pertinent question but the mere fact that we are asking it displays an enormously significant change in attitude.

Today the 'real' climbers are so far removed from the commercial circus on Everest that they might as well be regarded as participating in a completely different sport. These are the elite, by whom everyone else should be judging themselves. Instead, we have this strange schism in the sport with the elite quietly divorcing itself from what is happening on the eight-thousand-metre peaks almost as if they tacitly accept that it is not mountaineering.

At home, a General Election has just been fought with politicians struggling for survival, and with sleaze and corruption high on the agenda. A landslide victory for the New Labour Party and the unprecedented total rout of the Conservatives in both Scotland and Wales, suggests that perhaps the country has finally had enough of the lack of integrity. A 1995 MORI poll revealed that only three per cent of those asked felt that politics was a respectable career, which put those responsible for government in the same league as estate agents and journalists. Why do we expect politicians – those experts at looking deeply at the surface of things – to behave with honour, integrity and respect, to tell the truth and be loyal to their spouses? A politician today rarely resigns on points of principle or honour as once they did. If they behave badly, why should the rest of us behave well? If we take for granted that our leaders and our media are essentially self-serving and untrustworthy, what does it say about the nature of our society and why should we conduct ourselves any differently? If their motivation is money and power, why should that not also be ours?

A new season has opened on Everest since our return from Pumori. The hordes have once again massed in their tented villages amidst the moraines of the Khumbu and Rongbuk glaciers. Neither guides nor clients seem unduly perturbed by what happened twelve months ago. In an article by Peter Wilkinson in *Men's Journal* (U.S.), Jon Krakauer is reported saying that he sees no hope for better trained and more experienced clients, or more widespread use of smarter tactics: 'By '98, anything that was changed or learned will be forgotten. People have always died on Everest and always will. It will always appeal to people – not necessarily serious climbers – who just want to climb Everest. It's going to be guided, and there's no way it's going to be regulated.'

Many familiar faces have been seen again at the Everest base camps. Guy Cotter, who purchased Adventure Consultants from Rob Hall's widow, Jan Arnold, brought in a smaller than usual five-client expedition, but the price tag of $65,000 remains the same. Ed Viesturs, who topped out with the IMAX team in 1996, was this year an assistant guide for Cotter. Todd Burleson and Pete Athans, both of whom helped with the rescue efforts on the South Col last year, were also back on the mountain. The American film-maker David Breashears achieved his fourth ascent, while Athans and Viesturs each notched up a fifth. Twelve teams (including groups from the United States, Canada, Britain, Japan, Brazil, New Zealand, Malaysia and India) were issued with permits to attempt the mountain from the Nepalese side in the spring season of 1997. The numbers game, involving high risks and a great deal of money, has been in full swing again.

Casualty figures for the season include the deaths of three Russians of the Kazak Military Everest expedition, one German solo climber and a Sherpa in storms and falls on the north side of Everest. On the Nepalese side a Sherpa is reported to have died in a fall on the Lhotse face. At the beginning of May nine expeditions were poised for a summit attempt, waiting for the unusually stormy weather to calm down. By the end of the spring season in early June a total of 86 had succeeded in reaching the summit, and 8 died in the attempt. More by luck than judgement, no one was killed when a Nepalese army rescue helicopter crashed at base camp. Fortunately, after vehement protests, the landing site had been moved to one side, away from the climbers' tents where previously, to the consternation of their occupants, a wealthy Japanese (among others) had been flying in equipment and Sherpas.

Anatoli Boukreev, the phenomenal mountain guide from Kazakhstan, returned to climb the South Col route with an Indonesian-Russian expedition, this time acting not as a guide, but as 'the lead climbing consultant', lending his 'experience' to the team. It all sounds suspiciously like guiding to me. If he is paid for his services, then to all intents and purposes he is a guide. In 1996 Scott Fischer paid Boukreev the astonishingly generous fee of $25,000 for his services (most other guides receive between $10,000 and $15,000). Clearly business has not been diminished by the 1996 disaster. Boukreev now reports that he buried his friend Scott Fischer on the way up, as well as the body of Yasuko Namba on the South Col, using whatever small stones were available.

There are disturbing reports that Anatoli Boukreev might have found Bruce Herrod's body entangled in the fixed ropes just below the Hillary Step. Speaking to Todd Burleson at base camp, and later to Bikrum Pandey in Kathmandu, Boukreev said that it was difficult and frightening to have to climb over the body in such an exposed place in order to reach the foot of the Hillary Step. Presumably many more aspiring Everest climbers will have to do the same unless someone cuts the body free. He was by no means certain it was actually Herrod. At first he thought it could be Doug Hansen. Identification proved very difficult because of the body's condition after a year's exposure to the elements. Even the colour of the clothing had faded, making positive recognition so much harder. Besides, it makes little sense for Hansen to be found at that spot given that Breashears had climbed the mountain after Hansen's death and had found no one hanging on the ropes. In any case, Herrod made his climb after Breashears' ascent, and was the last person to die on the mountain that spring.

As far as is known there were no deaths that high on the South Col route in the 1996 autumn season, although three climbers were killed below the South Col. On 25 September, when Tom Richardson and I were retreating off Singu Chulu, a slab avalanche on the Lhotse face swept Scott Fischer's great friend, Lobsang Jangbu, to his death. Lobsang, a French climber and another Sherpa were killed as they climbed between Camp III and Camp IV at the start of their summit assault. An avalanche swamped them just below the Geneva Spur and hurled them down the Lhotse face. Lobsang leaves a two-month-old son and a young widow.

There is something unnerving about this carnage. I feel as if I am grasping at straws in an effort to understand why mountaineering ethical standards seem to have slipped to such low levels on Everest. There's a danger in finding reasons simply because one is looking for them. Himalayan climbing has become commercial, full stop. It is part of the mainstream tourist trade now. Whether you pay a company to act as your agent and organise the logistical side of the expedition, or you do it yourself, it is still going to cost a lot of money that has to be found somehow. The only expeditions not bedecked with sponsors' logos at Everest base camp are the commercial climbing companies who have no reliance on sponsors. Every other base camp team has tents, helmets, rucksacks and clothing plastered in every conceivable corporate logo. Does all this necessarily mean we are bound in the end to behave inhumanely? I cannot push from my mind those two incidents when climbers abandoned their fellow climbers to die alone and made no effort to give aid or comfort, however futile it may have seemed. For all the amazing feats of climbing on Everest in the past, and all the times when climbers have behaved so nobly and selflessly in their efforts to help others, these two incidents seem to have tarnished it all. No summit can ever be worth so much. No man should be able to witness such harrowing events and not be moved to help. Or am I biased, knowing how it feels to be left for dead?

I cannot deny that it was ambitions and ego that very nearly killed me eleven years ago on Siula Grande in Peru. Full of competitive zeal, I had gone to the Andes with my younger climbing partner, Simon Yates, hoping to tackle new routes, the harder the better, in Alpine-style. We did, and it nearly killed us. It is a style that has killed many of our friends. Although I sometimes compromise over the way in which I climb, I still feel in my heart that the only honest way is to do it in the purest style. However, that is my choice. It does not give me the right to enforce that view on others. In the same way, I can hope that people will behave well towards each other, but I cannot insist on it. There is no law to say that you must.

It sometimes seems unreal to have survived at all, having broken my leg in a short fall at six thousand metres. Simon made an extraordinary single-handed rescue attempt, only to be forced to cut me free from the rope linking us while he lowered me down the mountainside in a snowstorm. The second fall, one hundred and twenty feet into a crevasse with the severed rope following down on top of me, should have finished me off, and in the morning, hearing no response to his cries, Simon believed he had killed me.

Only the overwhelming desire not to die alone, slowly and without human company, kept me going until I got out of the crevasse and hopped and crawled down the glacier to where I had to believe our base camp was still occupied. Four and a half days it took to arrive within yards of where I thought our base camp had been. By then I was lost. I had given up hope. It never occurred to me to shout.

I didn't feel weak or tired, just empty. My body had slowed down but it was a gradual deterioration that I had not noticed. I had eaten nothing for four days and nights and I had lost nearly forty per cent of my body weight. The tell-tale, sickly stench of ketones hung on my breath, the saccharine smell of diabetics in an insulin coma. It was the result both of grave dehydration and of my body trying to absorb the proteins in the muscles and organs. My shattered knee was the least of my problems. I had run my course. I was going no further.

The snow fell intermittently from a dark sky. I had stopped looking at my watch and now had no idea of time passing. I muttered deliriously into the night and was answered by a sibilant wind and a sense of endless silence. I wanted someone to help me, to hold me, and the idea made me cry. I stopped when I smelt the faecal stench on my hands. It was the final straw. A pathetic and sordid way to die.

I could smell the warm, cloying stink of urine seeping through my sodden and torn pile salopettes. Under the tightly strapped sleeping mat which I had wrapped around my shattered right knee, I could feel warm fluid and wondered whether there was bleeding at the fracture site. My hands had become smeared in faeces, and although I recognised the sharp odour, it meant nothing to me. I couldn't understand where it had come from.

The dry river bed was half a mile wide, strewn with rocks and melt pools, and the river ran somewhere in the darkness. The tents were snuggled near a distinctive obelisk of granite. But where was I? Was I crawling towards the centre or back towards the glacier? I don't know how long it took for me to grasp the significance of the smell on my hands. Things happened so slowly that everything became disconnected.

When at last I decided to shout into the night, I was suddenly filled with dread. Would they be there? Why would they have waited so long for a dead man? It was now the start of the fifth day since I had broken my leg – four days since I last heard a voice, saw a face, saw any living thing. I remember hesitating, too scared to shout. If there was no answer, then I knew it was over. I was going alone.

The shout came out as a strangled cry. The clouds seemed to swallow the sound. I stared into the darkness, trying to guess where I should be looking. In the silence, wet snow-flakes caressed my face. My eyes began to burn. They had gone. The silence said it all. I was too late. I found myself pleading in breathless gasps . . . 'be there . . . you must be there . . . help me.' I remember crying like a child and feeling ashamed. I wanted it to end and I wanted someone to be there, anyone. There was only darkness and a heartless wind.

When I shouted again – more of a howl than a coherent sound – lights came on in the blackness, and a head torch spurted a sodium yellow light beam into the night, and I fell off my boulder and wept as heavy footfalls crunched in the gravel and voices shouted in the dark. Strong arms grabbed me and pulled me towards the lighted tents. Simon grinned and swore at me in shock – to see a dead man moving. He looked old and haggard and care-worn. After he had settled me gently against the soft down sleeping bags he zipped the tent door closed against the dark shadows of a frightening night.

Acknowledgements

During the writing of this book I was painfully aware that some of my views on the state of Himalayan climbing might upset some practitioners of the sport, not least those with a vested interest in it. It is not something I feel comfortable about doing but at the same time I am far from happy about the way Everest is being treated today.

I owe a debt of gratitude to all those friends who happily gave me their advice and criticism, especially members of the Pumori South Buttress Expedition to whom I should also extend my apologies for being such an impatient and irascible leader. Accounts of the 1996 Everest disaster by Michael Kennedy and Neal Beidleman in *Climbing*, and those by Jon Krakauer in *Outside*, *Esquire*, and *Time* magazines were invaluable. Conversations with Matt Dickinson, Simon Lowe, Henry Todd, Jon Tinker, Andy Parkin, Mal Duff, Guy Cotter, Richard Cowper, Simon Yates, Andy Perkins, Ian Tattersall, Ray Delaney, Audrey Salkeld, Bikrum Pandey, Xavier Eguskitza and others gave me advice and constructive criticism, some of which I agree with, and all of which made me think hard about what I was trying to say.

Karl Huyberechts kindly donated his photographs of the South Col, refusing any payment, and Christine Baxter Jones and Andy Parkin helped in tracing them. Richard Cowper, Ray Delaney, Ric Potter, Simon Lowe, Leo Dickinson, Simon Yates and Alison Reynolds also contributed photographs.

As always, Tony Colwell, my editor at Cape, gave me unstinting help and advice, and without his patient work I would never have been able to complete the book on time.

To all I offer my sincere thanks.

EVEREST (8848m)

SOUTH SUMMIT

NORTH EAST
RIDGE

SOUTH EAST
RIDGE

SOUTH WEST
FACE

SOUTH
COL

WEST RIDGE

WESTERN

KHUMBU ICEFALL

BASE CAMP